A Review of Taxes and Corporate Finance

A Review of Taxes and Corporate Finance

John R. Graham

Fuqua School of Business
Duke University
Durham, NC 27708-0120
and NBER

john.graham@duke.edu

the essence of knowledge

Boston – Delft

Foundations and Trends® in Finance

Published, sold and distributed by:
now Publishers Inc.
PO Box 1024
Hanover, MA 02339
USA
Tel. +1-781-985-4510
www.nowpublishers.com
sales@nowpublishers.com

Outside North America:
now Publishers Inc.
PO Box 179
2600 AD Delft
The Netherlands
Tel. +31-6-51115274

A Cataloging-in-Publication record is available from the Library of Congress

The preferred citation for this publication is J.R. Graham, A Review of Taxes and Corporate Finance, Foundation and Trends® in Finance, vol. 1, no. 7, pp. 573–691, 2006

Printed on acid-free paper

ISBN: 1-933019-41-7

Foundations and Trends® in Finance
Finance
Volume 1 Issue 7, 2006

Editorial Board

Editorial Scope

Foundations and Trends® in Finance will publish survey and tutorial articles in the following topics:

- Corporate Governance
- Corporate Financing
- Dividend Policy and Capital Structure
- Corporate Control
- Investment Policy
- Agency Theory and Information
- Market Microstructure
- Portfolio Theory
- Financial Intermediation
- Investment Banking
- Market Efficiency
- Security Issuance
- Anomalies and Behavioral Finance
- Asset-Pricing Theory
- Asset-Pricing Models
- Tax Effects
- Liquidity
- Equity Risk Premium
- Pricing Models and Volatility
- Fixed Income Securities
- Computational Finance
- Futures Markets and Hedging
- Financial Engineering
- Interest Rate Derivatives
- Credit Derivatives
- Financial Econometrics
- Estimating Volatilities and Correlations

Information for Librarians

Foundations and Trends® in Finance, 2006, Volume 1, 8 issues. ISSN paper version 1567-2395. ISSN online version 1567-2409. Also available as a combined paper and online subscription.

Foundations and Trends® in
Finance
Vol. 1, No. 7 (2006) 573–691

DOI: 10.1561/0500000010

now
the essence of knowledge

A Review of Taxes and Corporate Finance

John R. Graham[1]

[1] *Fuqua School of Business, Duke University, Durham, NC 27708-0120 and NBER, john.graham@duke.edu*

Abstract

This paper reviews domestic and multinational corporate tax research. For each topic, the theoretical arguments explaining how taxes can affect corporate decision-making and firm value are reviewed, followed by a summary of the related empirical evidence and a discussion of unresolved issues. Tax research generally supports the hypothesis that high-tax rate firms pursue policies that provide tax benefits. Many issues remain unresolved, however, including understanding whether tax effects are of first-order importance, why firms do not pursue tax benefits more aggressively, and whether corporate actions are affected by investor-level taxes.

Contents

Modigliani and Miller (1985) and Miller and Modigliani (1961) demonstrate that corporate financial decisions are irrelevant in a perfect, frictionless world. During the past 45 years, research has focused on whether financial decisions become relevant if capital markets are not perfect. This paper reviews the literature that investigates the consequences of allowing taxation, with emphasis on how taxes can affect corporate policies and firm value.[1] This role is potentially very important, given the sizable tax rates that many corporations and individuals face (see Fig. 1).

Modigliani and Miller (MM) argue that corporate financial policies do not add value in equilibrium, and therefore firm value equals the present value of operating cash flows. Once imperfections are introduced, however, corporate financial policies can affect firm value, and firms should pursue a given policy until the marginal benefit of doing so equals the marginal cost. A common theme in tax research involves expressing how various tax rules and regulations affect the marginal benefit of corporate actions. For example, when tax rules allow interest deductibility, a \$1 interest deduction provides tax savings of $\$1\text{x}\tau_C(.)$. $\tau_C(.)$ measures corporate marginal tax benefits and is a function of statutory tax rates, nondebt tax shields, the probability of experiencing a loss, international tax rules about dividend imputation and interest allocation, organizational form, and various other tax rules. A common theme that runs throughout this paper is the demonstration of how various tax rules affect the $\tau_C(.)$ benefit function, and therefore how they affect corporate incentives and decisions. A second but less common theme in tax research is related to how market imperfections affect costs. Given that this chapter reviews tax research, I emphasize research that describes how taxes affect costs and benefits – and only briefly discuss the influence of nontax factors.

There are multiple avenues for taxes to affect corporate decisions. Taxes can affect capital structure decisions (both domestic (Section 1)

[1] The interested reader can find excellent reviews of how taxes affect household investment decisions (Poterba, 2001) and the current state of tax research from the perspective of accountants (Shackelford and Shevlin, 2001) and public economists (Auerbach, 2002). Articles reviewing how nontax factors such as agency and informational imperfections affect corporate financial decisions can be found in the other chapters of this handbook.

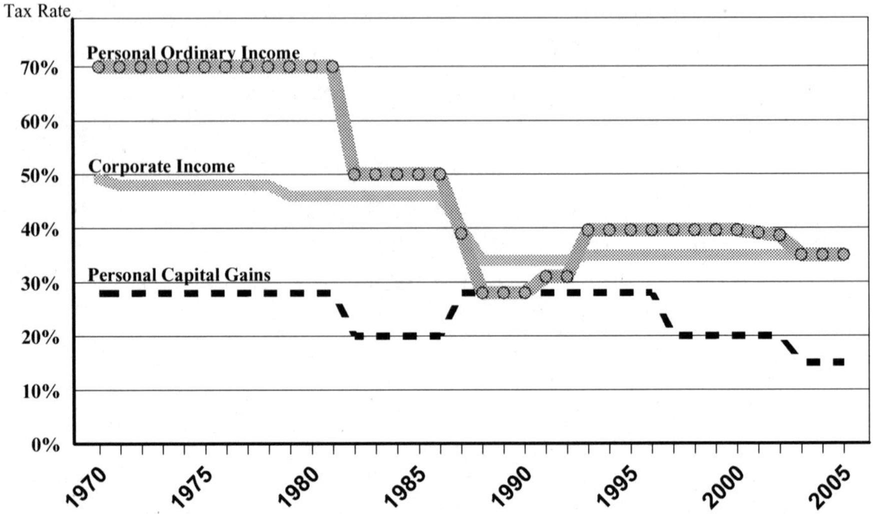

Fig. 1 Corporate and Personal Income Tax Rates
The highest tax bracket statutory rates are shown for individuals and C corporations. The corporate capital gains tax rate (not shown) was equal to the corporate income tax rate every rate after 1987. In May 2003 President Bush signed into law a reduction in the top personal income tax rate to 35%. This same law reduced top personal tax rates on capital gains and dividends to 15%. Source for pre-2003 numbers: Commerce Clearing House, annual publications.

and multinational (Section 2)), organizational form and restructurings (Section 3), payout policy (Section 4), compensation policy (Section 5),risk management (Section 6), and the use of tax shelters (Section 7). For each of these areas, the sections that follow provide a theoretical framework describing how taxes might affect corporate decisions, empirical predictions based on the theory, and summaries of the related empirical evidence. This approach is intended to highlight important questions about how taxes affect corporate decisions, and to summarize and critique the answers that have been thus far provided. Each section concludes with a discussion of unanswered questions and possible avenues for future research. Overall, substantial progress has been made investigating if and how taxes affect corporate financial decisions – but much work remains to be done. Section 8 concludes and proposes directions for future research.

1

Taxes and Capital Structure – U.S. Tax System

1.1 Theory and empirical predictions

This section reviews capital structure research related to the "classical" tax system found in the United States. (Section 2 reviews multinational and imputation tax systems.) The key features of the classical system are that corporate income is taxed at a rate τ_C, interest is deductible and so is paid out of income before taxes, and equity payout is not deductible but is paid from the residual remaining after corporate taxation. In this tax system, interest, dividends, and capital gains income are taxed upon receipt by investors (at tax rates τ_P, $\tau_{div}=\tau_P$, and τ_G, respectively). Most of the research assumes that equity is the marginal source of funds and that dividends are paid according to a fixed payout policy.[1] To narrow the discussion, I assume that regulations or transactions costs prevent investors from following the tax-avoidance schemes implied by Miller and Scholes (1978), in which investors borrow via insurance or other tax-free vehicles to avoid personal tax on interest or dividend income.

[1] This assumption implies that retained earnings are not "trapped equity" that is implicitly taxed at the dividend tax rate, even while still retained. See Auerbach (2002) for more on the trapped equity or "new" view.

In this framework, the after-personal-tax value to investors of a corporation paying \$1 of interest is $\$1(1 - \tau_P)$. In contrast, if that capital were instead returned as equity income, it would be subject to taxation at both the corporate and personal level, and the investor would receive $\$1(1 - \tau_C)(1 - \tau_E)$. The equity tax rate, τ_E, is often modeled as a blended dividend and capital gains tax rate.[2] The net tax advantage of \$1 of debt payout, relative to \$1 of equity payout, is

$$(1 - \tau_P) - (1 - \tau_C)(1 - \tau_E). \tag{1.1}$$

If expression (1.1) is positive, debt interest is the tax-favored way to return capital to investors, once both corporate and individual taxation are considered. In this case, to maximize firm value, there is a tax incentive to issue debt instead of equity.

Eq. (1.1) captures the benefit of a firm paying \$1 as debt interest in the current period, relative to paying \$1 as equity income. If a firm has \$D of debt with coupon rate r_D, the net benefit of using debt rather than equity is

$$[(1 - \tau_P) - (1 - \tau_C)(1 - \tau_E)]r_D D. \tag{1.2}$$

Given this expression, the value of a firm with debt can be written as

$$\begin{aligned} \mathit{Value}_{\text{with debt}} = {} & \mathit{Value}_{\text{no debt}} \\ & + PV[(1 - \tau_P) - (1 - \tau_C)(1 - \tau_E)]r_D D \end{aligned} \tag{1.3}$$

where the PV term measures the present value of all current and future interest deductions. Note that eq. (1.3) implicitly assumes that using debt adds tax benefits but has no other effect on incentives, operations or value.[3]

MM (1958) is the seminal capital structure paper. If capital markets are perfect, τ_C, τ_P and τ_E all equal zero, and it does not matter whether the firm finances with debt or equity (i.e.,

[2] In mid-2003 the tax rate on both dividends and capital gains were reduced to 15% for individual investors, thereby simplifying and greatly reducing the level of equity taxation relative to historic levels.

[3] There are other approaches to modeling the tax benefits of debt that do not fit directly into this general framework. For example, Goldstein et al. (2001) develop a dynamic contingent-claims model in which firms can restructure debt. They estimate that the tax benefits of debt should equal between eight and nine percent of firm value. See Goldstein et al. for references to other contingent-claims models.

$Value_{\text{with debt}} = Value_{\text{no debt}}$). That is, the value of the firm equals the value of equity plus the value of debt – but total value is not affected by the proportions of debt and equity. I use this implication as the null throughout the capital structure discussion.

Null hypotheses

- Firms do not have optimal tax-driven capital structures.
- The value of a firm with debt is equal to the value of an identical firm without debt (i.e., there is no net tax advantage to debt).

In their "correction article," MM (1963) consider corporate income taxation but continue to assume that τ_P and τ_E equal zero. In this case, the second term in eq. (1.3) collapses to PV[$\tau_C r_D$D]: Because interest is deductible, paying \$$r_D$D of interest saves $\tau_C r_D$D in taxes each period relative to returning capital as equity. MM (1963) assume that interest deductions are as risky as the debt that generates them and should be discounted by r_D.[4] With perpetual debt, MM (1963) argue that the value of a firm with debt financing is

$$V_{\text{with debt}} = V_{\text{no debt}} + \frac{\tau_C r_D D}{r_D} = V_{\text{no debt}} + \tau_C D, \qquad (1.4)$$

where the τ_CD term represents the tax advantage of debt. Note that eq. (1.4) contains a term that captures the tax benefit of using debt (τ_CD) but no offsetting cost of debt term. Eq. (1.4) has two strong implications. First, corporations should finance with 100% debt because the marginal benefit of debt is τ_C, which is often assumed to be a positive constant. Second, if τ_C is constant, firm value increases (linearly) with D due to tax benefits.

[4] The assumption that debt should be discounted at r_D is controversial because it requires the amount of debt to remain fixed. Miles and Ezzell (1985) demonstrate that if the dollar amount of debt is not fixed but instead is set to maintain a target debt-equity ratio, then interest deductions have equity risk and should be discounted with the return on assets, r_A, rather than r_D. (Miles and Ezzell, 1985 allow first period financing to be fixed, which requires adjusting the discount factor by $(1 + r_A)/(1 + r_D)$). In contrast, Grinblatt and Titman (2002) argue that firms often pay down debt when things are going well and stock returns are high, and do not alter debt when returns are low. Such behavior can produce a low or negative beta for debt and hence a low discount rate for the tax benefits of debt. In either the Miles and Ezzell or Grinblatt and Titman case, however, the value of a levered firm still equals the value of the unlevered firm plus a "coefficient times debt" term – the discounting controversy only affects the coefficient.

The first implication was recognized as extreme, so researchers developed models that relax the MM (1958) assumptions and consider costs of debt. In the early models, firms trade-off the tax benefits of debt with costs. The first cost proposed in the literature was the cost of bankruptcy, or more generally, costs of financial distress. Kraus and Litzenberger (1973) show in a state-preference framework that firms should trade-off bankruptcy costs with the tax benefits of debt to arrive at an optimal capital structure that involves less than 100% debt. Scott (1976) shows the same with continuous variables. The bankruptcy cost solution does not appear empirically to ex ante offset the benefits of debt.[5] Therefore other papers have proposed non-bankruptcy costs that could be traded off against the tax benefits of debt. For example, Jensen and Meckling (1976) introduce agency costs of equity and leverage-related deadweight costs.[6] Myers (1977) introduces underinvestment costs that can result from too much "debt overhang."

Regardless of the type of cost, the basic trade-off implications remain similar to those in MM (1963): 1) the incentive to finance with debt increases with the corporate tax rate, and 2) firm value increases with the use of debt (up to the point where the marginal cost equals the marginal benefit of debt). Note also that in these models, different firms can have different optimal debt ratios depending on the relative costs and benefits of debt (i.e., depending on differing firm characteristics).

Prediction 1 All else constant, for taxable firms, value increases with the use of debt because of tax benefits (up to the point where the marginal cost equals the marginal benefit of debt).

---

[5] Warner (1977) shows that direct costs of bankruptcy average no more than 5.3% ex post in railroad bankruptcies. More recently, Andrade and Kaplan (1998) show that the ex post costs of distress brought about by financing choice amount to 20% of firm value for a group of industrial firms. Miller (1977) notes that firms choose optimal debt policy by considering ex ante costs of distress, so ex ante costs are measured by multiplying the costs mentioned above need by the conditional probability of distress. Miller points out that ex ante costs of financial distress appear to be very small compared to the apparently large tax benefits of debt.

[6] Parrino and Weisbach (1999) use simulations to conclude that the agency costs of debt are too small to offset the tax benefits, and Esty (1998) empirically examines the effects of agency costs on capital structure in the banking industry.

Prediction 2 Corporations have a tax incentive to finance with debt that increases with the corporate marginal tax rate. All else equal, this implies that firms have differing optimal debt ratios if their tax rates differ.

Prediction 1 is based directly on eq. (1.4), while Prediction 2 is based on the first derivative of eq. (1.4) with respect to D.

Miller (1977) argues that personal taxes can eliminate the "100% debt" implication, without the need for bankruptcy or agency costs. (Farrar and Selwyn, 1967 took first steps in this direction.) Miller's argument is that the marginal costs of debt and equity, net of the effects of personal and corporate taxes, should be equal in equilibrium, so firms are indifferent between the two financing sources. In essence, the corporate tax savings from debt is offset by the personal tax disadvantage to investors from holding debt, relative to holding equity. All else equal (including risk), this personal tax disadvantage causes investors to demand higher pretax returns on debt, relative to equity returns. From the firm's perspective, paying this higher pretax return wipes out the tax advantage of using debt financing.

Fig. 1.1 illustrates Miller's point. The horizontal line in Panel A depicts the supply curve for debt; the line is horizontal because Miller assumes that the benefit of debt for all firms equals a fixed constant τ_C. The demand for debt curve is initially horizontal at zero, representing demand by tax-free investors, but eventually slopes upward because the return on debt must increase to attract investors with higher personal income tax rates. By making the simplifying assumption that $\tau_E = 0$, Miller's equilibrium is reached when the marginal investor with $\tau_P^* = \tau_C$ is attracted to purchase debt. In this equilibrium, the entire surplus (the area between the supply and demand curves) accrues to investors subject to personal tax rates less than τ_P^*.

There are several implications from Miller's (1977) analysis. The first two are new:

Prediction 3 High personal taxes on interest income (relative to personal taxes on equity income) are negatively related to the corporate use of debt.

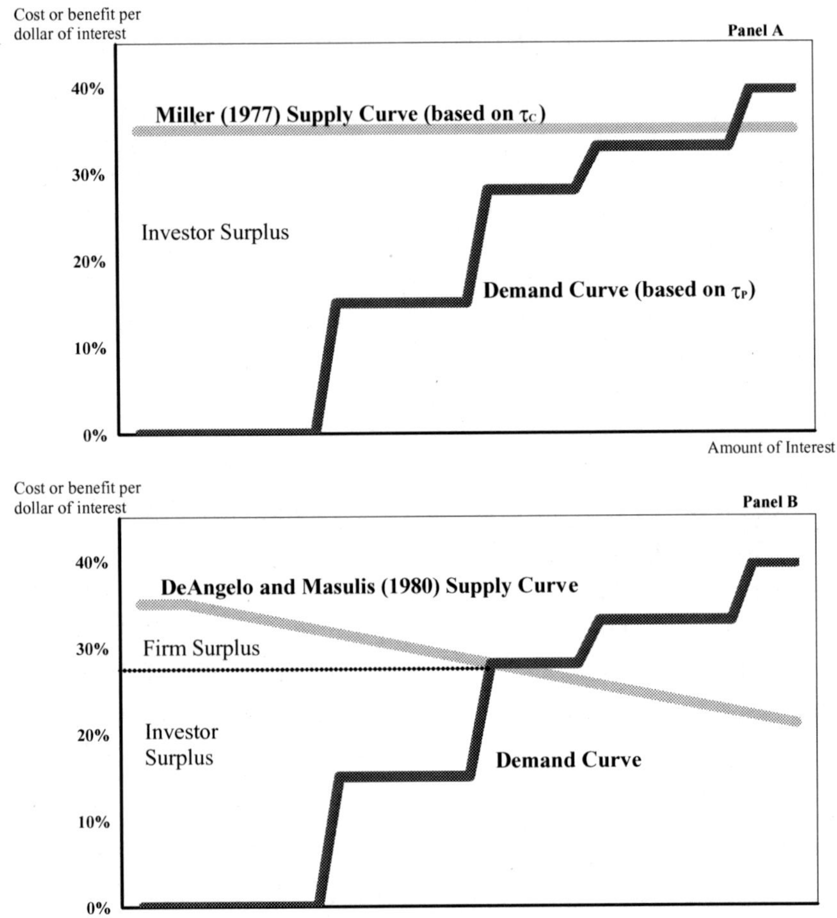

Fig. 1.1 Equilibrium Supply and Demand Curves for Corporate Debt
The supply curve depicts the expected tax rate (and therefore the tax benefit of a dollar of interest) for firms that issue debt. The demand curve shows the tax rate (and therefore the tax cost of a dollar of interest) for investors who purchase debt. The tax rates for the marginal supplier and marginal investor are determined by the intersection of the two curves. In the Miller Equilibrium (panel A), all firms have the same tax rate in every state, so the supply curve is flat. The demand curve slopes upward because tax-free investors are the initial purchasers of corporate bonds, followed by low-tax-rate investors, and eventually followed by high-tax-rate-investors. All investors with tax rate less than the marginal investor's (i.e., investors with tax rates of 33% or less in Panel A) enjoy "investor surplus" in the form of an after-tax return on debt higher than their reservation return. In Panel B, the supply curve is downward sloping because firms differ in the probability of full utilization of interest deductions (or have varying amounts of nondebt tax shields), and therefore have differing benefits of interest deductibility. Firms with tax rates higher than that for the marginal supplier of date (i.e., firms with tax rates greater than 28% in Panel B) enjoy "firm surplus" because the benefit of interest deductibility is larger than the personal tax cost implicit in the debt interest rate.

Prediction 4 The aggregate supply of debt is affected by relative corporate and personal taxes.

The other implications are consistent with the null hypotheses stated above: 1) there is no net tax advantage to debt at the corporate level (once one accounts for the higher debt yields that investors demand because of the relatively high personal taxes associated with receiving interest), 2) though taxes affect the aggregate supply of debt in equilibrium, they do not affect the optimal capital structure for any particular firm (i.e., it does not matter which particular firms issue debt, as long as aggregate supply equals aggregate demand), and 3) using debt does not increase firm value.

A general version of Miller's argument (that does not assume $\tau_E = 0$) can be expressed in terms of eq. (1.3). Once personal taxes are introduced into this framework, the appropriate discount rate is measured after-personal income taxes to capture the (after-personal-tax) opportunity cost of investing in debt. In this case, the value of a firm using perpetual debt is:[7]

$$
\begin{aligned}
V_{\text{with debt}} &= V_{\text{no debt}} + \frac{[(1-\tau_P) - (1-\tau_C)(1-\tau_E)]r_D D}{(1-\tau_P)r_D} \\
&= V_{\text{no debt}} + \left[1 - \frac{(1-\tau_C)(1-\tau_E)}{(1-\tau_P)}\right] D. \qquad (1.5)
\end{aligned}
$$

If the investor-level tax on interest income (τ_P) is large relative to tax rates on corporate and equity income (τ_C and τ_E), the net tax advantage of debt can be zero or even negative. Note that eq. (1.5) is identical to eq. (1.4) if there are no personal taxes, or if $\tau_P = \tau_E$.

One way that eq. (1.5) can be an equilibrium expression is for the right-most term in eq. (1.5) to equal zero in equilibrium (e.g., $(1 - \tau_P) = (1 - \tau_C)(1 - \tau_E)$), in which case the implications from Miller (1977) are unchanged. Alternatively, the tax benefit term in eq. (1.5) can be positive and a separate cost term can be introduced in the spirit

[7] See Sick (1990), Taggart (1991), or Benninga and Sarig (1997) for derivation of expressions like eq. (1.5) under various discounting assumptions. These expressions are of the form $V_{\text{with debt}} = V_{\text{no debt}} + \text{coefficient}^* D$, with the coefficient an increasing (decreasing) function of corporate (personal income) tax rates.

of the trade-off models; in this case, the corporate incentive to issue debt and firm value both increase with $[1 - (1 - \tau_C)(1 - \tau_E)/(1 - \tau_P)]$ and firm-specific optimal debt ratios can exist. The bracketed expression specifies the degree to which personal taxes (Prediction 3) offset the corporate incentive to use debt (Prediction 2). Recall that τ_P and τ_E are personal tax rates for the marginal investor(s), and therefore are difficult to pin down empirically (more on this in Section 1.4).

DeAngelo and Masulis (1980; hereafter DM) broaden Miller's (1977) model and put the focus on the marginal tax benefit of debt, represented above by τ_C. DM argue that $\tau_C(.)$ is not constant and always equal to the statutory rate. Instead, $\tau_C(.)$ is a function that decreases in nondebt tax shields (e.g., depreciation and investment tax credits) because nondebt tax shields (NDTS) crowd out the tax benefit of interest. Further, Kim (1989) highlights that firms do not always benefit fully from incremental interest deductions, for example when taxable income is negative. This implies that $\tau_C(.)$ is a decreasing function of a firm's debt usage because existing interest deductions reduce the tax benefit of incremental interest.

Modeling $\tau_C(.)$ as a function has important implications because the supply of debt function can become downward sloping (see Panel B in Fig. 1.1). This implies that there is a corporate advantage to using debt, as measured by the "firm surplus" of issuing debt (the area above the dotted line but below the supply curve in Panel B). Moreover, high-tax-rate firms supply debt (i.e., are on the portion of the supply curve to the left of its intersection with demand), which implies that there can exist tax-driven firm-specific optimal debt ratios (as in Prediction 2), and that the tax benefits of debt add value for high-tax-rate firms (as in Prediction 1). The DeAngelo and Masulis (1980) approach leads to the following prediction, which expands Prediction 2:

Prediction 2' All else equal, to the extent that they reduce $\tau_C(.)$, nondebt tax shields and/or interest deductions from already-existing debt reduce the tax incentive to use debt. Similarly, the tax incentive to use debt decreases with the probability that a firm will experience nontaxable states of the world.

1.2 Empirical evidence on whether the tax advantage of debt increases firm value

Prediction 1 indicates that the tax benefits of debt add τ_CD (eq. (1.4)) or $[1-(1-\tau_C)(1-\tau_E)/(1-\tau_P)]D$ (eq. (1.5)) to firm value. If $\tau_C =$ 40% and the debt ratio is 35%, eq. (1.4) indicates that the contribution of taxes to firm value is about 14% ($0.14 = \tau_C$ x debt-to-value). This tax benefit would be offset by costs and other factors that reduce the corporate tax benefit of interest deductibility, such as personal taxes, nontax costs of debt, and the possibility that interest deductions are not fully valued in every state of the world. This section reviews empirical research that attempts to quantify the net tax benefits of debt. The first group of papers studies market reactions to exchange offers, which should net out the various costs and benefits of debt. The remainder of the section reviews recent analyses based on large-sample regressions and concludes by examining explicit benefit functions for interest deductions.

1.2.1 Exchange offers

To investigate whether the tax benefits of debt increase firm value (Prediction 1), Masulis (1980) examines exchange offers made during the 1960s and 1970s. Because one security is issued and another simultaneously retired in an exchange offer, Masulis argues that exchanges hold investment policy relatively constant and are primarily changes in capital structure. Masulis' tax hypothesis is that leverage-increasing (−decreasing) exchange offers increase (decrease) firm value because they increase (decrease) tax deductions. Note that Masulis implicitly assumes that firms are underlevered. In reality, for a company already at its optimum, a movement in either direction (i.e., increasing or decreasing debt) would decrease firm value.

Masulis (1980) finds evidence consistent with his predictions: leverage-increasing exchange offers increase equity value by 7.6%, and leverage-decreasing transactions decrease value by 5.4%. Moreover, the exchange offers with the largest increases in tax deductions (debt-for-common and debt-for-preferred) have the largest positive stock price reactions (9.8% and 4.7%, respectively). Using a similar sample, Masulis (1983) regresses stock returns on the change in debt in exchange offers and finds a debt coefficient of approximately 0.40 (which is statistically indistinguishable from the top statutory corporate tax rate during that era). This is consistent with tax deductions increasing firm value as in eq. (1.4) (and also consistent with some alternative hypotheses discussed below) but it is surprising because such a large coefficient implies near-zero personal tax and non-tax costs to debt. That is, the debt coefficient in Masulis (1983) measures the average benefit of debt (averaged across firms and averaged over the incremental net benefit of each dollar of debt for a given firm) *net of the costs*. An average net benefit of 0.40 requires that the costs are much smaller than the benefits for most dollars of debt. For the post-exchange offer capital structure to satisfy the MB = MC equilibrium condition, the benefit or cost curves (or both) must be very steeply sloped near their intersection.

Myers (1984) and Cornett and Travlos (1989) argue that Masulis' (1980) hypothesis is problematic. If firms optimize, they should only adjust capital structure to move towards an optimal debt ratio, whether that involves increasing debt or equity. In other words, increasing debt will not always add to firm value, even if interest reduces tax liabilities. Graham et al. (1999) point out that if a firm starts at its optimal capital structure, it will only perform an exchange offer if something moves the firm out of equilibrium. They derive conditions under which stock-price-maximizing exchanges are unrelated to marginal tax rates because market reactions aggregate tax and non-tax informational aspects of capital structure changes. Therefore, nontax reactions might explain Masulis' (1980) results. As described next, several papers have found evidence of non-tax factors affecting exchange offer market reactions. It is important to note that these post-Masulis papers do not prove that the tax interpretation is wrong – but they do offer alternative interpretations.

First, some papers find evidence of positive (negative) stock reactions to leverage-increasing (leverage-decreasing) events that are unrelated to tax deductions: Asquith and Mullins (1986), Masulis and Korwar (1986), and Mikkelson and Partch (1986) find negative stock price reactions to straight equity issuance, and Pinegar and Lease

(1986) find positive stock price reactions to preferred-for-common exchanges. Second, Mikkelson and Partch (1986) and Eckbo (1986) find that straight debt issuance (without equity retirement) produces a stock price reaction that is indistinguishable from zero. Third, some papers find that exchange offers convey non-tax information that affects security prices, perhaps due to asymmetric information problems along the lines suggested by Myers and Majluf (1984) or due to signaling (Ross, 1977 and Leland and Pyle, 1977). For example, Shah (1994) correlates exchange offers with information about reduced future cash flows (for leverage-decreasing offers) and decreased risk (for leverage-increasing offers). Finally, Cornett and Travlos (1989) provide evidence that weakens Masulis' (1983) conclusions. Cornett and Travlos regress event stock returns on the change in debt and two variables that control for information effects (the ex-post change in inside ownership and ex-post abnormal earnings). They find the coefficient on the change in debt variable is insignificant while the coefficients on the other variables are significant, which implies that the positive stock price reaction is related to positive information conveyed by the exchange.[8] Cornett and Travlos conclude that equity-for-debt exchanges convey information about the future – but find no evidence of increased value due to tax benefits.

Two recent papers examine the exchange of traditional preferred stock for monthly income preferred stock (MIPS). These two securities differ primarily in terms of their tax characteristics, so any market reaction should have minimal non-tax explanations. MIPS interest is tax deductible for corporations (like debt interest) and preferred dividends are not. On the investor side, corporate investors enjoy a 70% dividends received deduction (DRD) for preferred dividends but recipients of MIPS interest receive no parallel deduction.[9] When issuing MIPS to retire preferred, corporations gain the tax benefit of interest

[8] Cornett and Travlos do not report whether they get a significant positive tax coefficient (like Masulis, 1983 did) when they exclude the information variables. Therefore, their results could be driven by their using a different sample than used by Masulis.

[9] A 70% DRD means that a corporation that owns another firm's stock only pays tax on 30% of the dividends received. Note that evidence in Erickson and Maydew (1998) implies that corporations are the marginal investor in preferred stock (see footnote 28).

deductibility but experience two costs: underwriting costs, and possibly an increased coupon due to the personal tax penalty (because investors are fully taxed on MIPS interest in contrast to corporate investors receiving the DRD on preferred dividends). Engel and Maydew (1999) compare MIPS yields to preferred yields and conclude that the tax benefit of MIPS are approximately \$0.28 per dollar of face value, net of the aforementioned costs. Irvine and Rosenfeld (2000) use abnormal announcement returns to estimate the value at \$0.26. Given that MIPS and preferred are nearly identical in all legal and informational respects, these studies provide straight-forward evidence of the positive contribution of taxes to firm value, net of underwriting and personal tax costs. Nayar (2005) finds that when the IRS denied (restored) interest deductibility for LYONS, an instrument similar to MIPS, firm value fell (increased) in recognition of the loss (gain) of interest tax deductions.

1.2.2 Cross-sectional regressions

Fama and French (1998; hereafter FF) attempt to estimate eq. (1.4) and Prediction 1 directly, by regressing V_L on debt interest, dividends, and a proxy for V_U. They argue that a positive coefficient on interest is evidence of positive tax benefits of debt. FF measure V_L as the excess of market value over book assets. They proxy V_U with a collection of control variables including current earnings, assets, and R&D spending, as well as future changes in these same variables. (All the variables in the regression are deflated by assets.) If these control variables adequately proxy for V_U, the regression coefficient on interest will measure the tax benefit of debt (which is hypothesized to be positive). The main difficulty with this approach is that if the control variables measure V_U with error, the regression coefficients can be biased. FF perform a series of regressions on a broad cross-section of firms, using both level-form and first-difference specifications. In all cases, the coefficient on interest is either insignificant or negative. Fama and French interpret their results as being inconsistent with debt tax benefits having a first-order effect on firm value. Instead, they argue that interest provides information about earnings that is not otherwise captured by their controls for V_U. In other words9 V_U is measured with error, which results in the interest coefficient picking up a negative valuation effect related to financial distress or some other cost.

Kemsley and Nissim (2002) attempt to circumvent this measurement problem. They perform a switch of variables, moving the earnings variable (which they assume proxies V_U with error) to the left-hand side of the regression and V_L to the right-side. Their regression tests the relation $V_U = V_L - \text{coeff} * \text{D}$.

When Kemsley and Nissim regress EBIT on V_L and debt, the debt coefficient is negative, which they interpret as evidence that debt contributes to firm value. The coefficient also changes through time in proportional to changes in statutory tax rates. In my opinion, the Kemsley and Nissim analysis should be interpreted carefully. First, their regression specification can be interpreted as measuring the effect of debt on earnings just as well as it can be interpreted as a switch-of-variables that fixes a measurement error problem in Fama and French (1998). Second, the debt coefficient has the correct sign for the full sample only in a nonlinear specification in which all the right-hand side variables are interacted with a crude measure of the discount rate. Finally, the coefficient that measures the net benefit of debt has an absolute value of 0.40. While consistent with Masulis (1983), such a large coefficient implies near-zero average debt costs and a near-zero effect of personal taxes.

1.2.3 Marginal benefit functions

Using a different approach, Graham (2000, 2001) simulates interest deduction benefit functions and uses them to estimate the tax-reducing value of each incremental dollar of interest expense. For a given level of interest deductions, Graham essentially integrates over possible states of the world (i.e., both taxable and nontaxable states) to determine a firm's expected τ_C, which specifies the expected tax benefit of an incremental dollar of interest deduction. Marginal tax benefits of debt decline as more debt is added because the probability increases with each incremental dollar of interest that the next dollar will not be fully valued in every state of the world. Using simulation methods (described more fully in Section 1.3.2) and various levels of interest deductions,

Graham maps out firm-specific interest benefit functions analogous to the supply of debt curve in Panel B of Fig. 1.1.

By integrating under these benefit functions, Graham (2000) estimates that the tax benefit of debt equals approximately 9–10% of firm value during 1980–1994 (ignoring all costs), and Graham (2006) finds that the tax benefit of debt is 7.8%, 9.8%, 9.1%, 9.5%, and 7.7% of firm value in 1995–1999, respectively (see Table 1.1). The fact that these figures are less than the 14% estimated (at the beginning of Section 1) with the back of the envelope "τ_CD" calculation reflects the reduced value of interest deductions in some states of the world. When personal taxes are considered, the tax benefit of debt falls to 7–8% of firm value during 1980–1994 (i.e., this is Graham's estimate of the "firm surplus" in Panel B of Fig. 1.1).

Graham also estimates the "money left on the table" that firms could obtain if they levered up to the point where their last dollar of interest deduction is valued at the full statutory tax rate (i.e., the "kink," which is the point just before incremental tax benefits begin to decline).[10] Graham (2006) updates the money left on the table calculations in Graham (2000, his Figure 1.1). If all firms lever up to operate at the kink in their benefit functions, they could add 10.5% to firm value over the 1995–1999 period (see Table 1.1). This number can be interpreted either as a measure of the value loss due to conservative corporate debt policy, or as a lower bound for the difficult-to-measure costs of debt that would occur if a company were to lever up to its kink. In the former interpretation, these estimates imply that large tax benefits of debt appear to go unexploited, and that large, profitable firms (which would seem to face the lowest costs of debt) are the most conservative in their use of debt.[11] In general, these implications are hard

[10] For example, if during 1995–1999 all firms levered up to just before the point of declining benefit, simulations performed for this paper indicate that the average company would have total tax benefits of debt of around 18% of firm value. That is, by levering up, the typical firm could add interest deductions with tax benefit equal to 10% of firm value, above and beyond their current level of tax benefits.

[11] McDonald (2004) argues that the prevalence of writing puts or purchasing calls on their own shares is also evidence that many firms pass up potential interest deductions. For example, writing a put (which involves implicit borrowing) can be replicated by explicitly borrowing today to purchase a share on the open market and repaying the loan in the future. The cash flows are identical in these two strategies but the latter results in the

Table 1.1 Annual calculations of the mean benefits of debt and degree of debt conservatism

Before-financing MTR is the mean Graham (1996a) simulated corporate marginal tax rate based on earnings before interest deductions, and *after-financing MTR* is the same based on earnings after interest deductions. *Kink* is the multiple by which interest payments could increase without a firm experiencing reduced marginal benefit on incremental deductions (i.e., the amount of interest at the point at which a firm's marginal benefit function becomes downward sloping, divided by actual interest expense) as in Graham (2000). The *tax benefit of debt* is the reduction in corporate and state tax liabilities occurring because interest expense is tax deductible, expressed as a percentage of firm value. *Money left on the table* is the additional tax benefit that could be obtained, ignoring all costs, if firms with kink greater than one increased their interest deductions in proportion with kink.

	Before-financing MTR	After-financing MTR	Kink	Tax benefit of debt	Money left on table
1980	0.415	0.324	3.10	10.1	27.7
1981	0.413	0.319	2.98	11.4	28.6
1982	0.397	0.286	2.69	11.0	23.2
1983	0.388	0.282	2.68	10.7	22.5
1984	0.380	0.275	2.75	10.9	21.6
1985	0.366	0.255	2.51	11.1	21.8
1986	0.356	0.241	2.39	11.6	20.5
1987	0.296	0.198	2.35	10.7	19.5
1988	0.259	0.172	2.30	9.9	16.7
1989	0.258	0.169	2.24	10.6	15.8
1990	0.258	0.164	2.08	10.7	15.3
1991	0.257	0.160	1.99	9.6	11.7
1992	0.258	0.165	2.07	8.7	9.7
1993	0.236	0.175	1.71	7.7	8.0
1994	0.249	0.183	1.94	7.3	8.5
1995	0.260	0.207	1.99	7.8	9.8
1996	0.261	0.185	2.05	9.8	12.2
1997	0.261	0.188	2.08	9.1	10.9
1998	0.252	0.165	2.00	9.5	10.7
1999	0.252	0.170	1.90	7.7	8.9

for a trade-off model to explain. Graham (2000), Lemmon and Zender (2001) and Minton and Wruck (2001) try to identify nontax costs that are large enough in a trade-off sense that perhaps these firms are not in fact underlevered.

To sum up, a fair amount of research has found evidence consistent with tax benefits adding to firm value. However, some of this evidence is ambiguous because non-tax explanations or econometric issues cloud

firm receiving a tax deduction. The fact that many firms write puts is consistent with them passing up interest tax deductions.

interpretation. Additional research in three specific areas would be helpful. First, we need more market-based research along the lines of the MIPs exchanges, where tax effects are isolated from information and other factors and therefore the interpretation is fairly unambiguous. Second, additional cross-sectional regression research that investigates the market value of the tax benefits of debt would be helpful in terms of clarifying or confirming the interpretation of existing cross-sectional regression analysis. Finally, if the tax benefits of debt do in fact add to firm value, an important unanswered question is why firms do not use more debt, especially large, profitable firms.[12] We need to better understand whether this implies that some firms are not optimizing, or whether there are costs and other influences that have not been adequately modeled in previous research.

Regarding this last point, several papers discussed later in this review address Graham's (2000) use of public financial statement (i.e., Compustat). If there are sufficient "off balance sheet" deductions, not available to a Compustat researcher, then debt interest deductions might be less valuable than implied in Graham (2000), and correspondingly firms might not be as underlevered either. Graham et al. (2004) consider stock option deductions, Stefanascu defined benefit pension obligations, and Graham and Tucker (2006) tax shelters, and all three papers find that this would reduce the apparent underleveage relative to that measured with Compustat. However, Graham and Mills (2006) use tax return data and find that even when all deductions are considered, including those not publically available, the degree of underleverage remains large. Some papers (e.g., Hennessey and Whited, 2005 respond that dynamic considerations could lead to firms preserving debt capacity, and therefore small debt ratios not being suboptimal. Almeida and Phillipon (2005) argue that present value of distress might be larger than previously mentioned (due to the wrong discount rate being use previously), thereby justifying small debt ratios. Berk et al. (2006) show that the loss of human capital adds to the costs of barnkruptcy, and therefore argue that bankrupcy costs might be of

[12] Shyum-Sunder and Myers (1999), Lemmon and Zender (2002), Leary and Roberts (2005, 2006), and related papers investigate whether the trade-off model is the correct model of capital structure, which has implications towards interpreting these results.

the same order of magnitude as tax benefits. Even these arguments, however, do not fully explain the cross-sectional puzzle from Graham (2000) that firms that would appear to have the lowest costs of debt also have the highest unexploited benefits (that is, marginal benefit appears to exceed marginal cost). More research is needed to address this issue.

1.3 Empirical evidence on whether corporate taxes affect debt vs. equity policy

Trade-off models imply that firms should issue debt as long as the marginal benefit of doing so (measured by τ_C) is larger than the marginal cost. $\tau_C(.)$ is a decreasing function of nondebt tax shields, existing debt tax shields, and the probability of experiencing losses, so the incentive to use debt declines with these three factors (Prediction 2'). In general, high-tax rate firms should use more debt than low-tax rate firms (Prediction 2). The papers reviewed in this section generally use reduced-form cross-sectional or panel regressions to test these predictions – and ignore personal taxes altogether. For expositional reasons, I start with tests of Prediction 2'.

1.3.1 Nondebt tax shields, profitability, and the use of debt

Bradley et al. (1984) perform one of the early regression tests for tax effects along the lines suggested by DeAngelo and Masulis (1980). Bradley et al. regress firm-specific debt-to-value ratios on nondebt tax shields (as measured by depreciation plus investment tax credits), R&D expense, the time-series volatility of EBITDA, and industry dummies. The tax hypothesis is that nondebt tax shields are negatively related to debt usage because they substitute for interest deductions (Prediction 2'). However, Bradley et al. find that debt is positively related to nondebt tax shields, opposite the tax prediction. This surprising finding, and others like it, prompted Stewart Myers (1984) to state in his presidential address to the American Finance Association, (p. 588) "I know of no study clearly demonstrating that a firm's tax status has predictable, material effects on its debt policy. I think the wait for such a study will be protracted."

One problem with using nondebt tax shields, in the form of depreciation and investment tax credits, to explain debt policy is that nondebt tax shields are positively correlated with profitability and investment. If profitable (i.e., high-tax rate) firms invest heavily and also borrow to fund this investment, this can induce a positive relation between debt and nondebt tax shields and overwhelm the tax substitution between interest and nondebt tax shields (Dammon and Senbet, 1988, Dotan and Ravid, 1985). Another issue is that nondebt tax shields (as well as existing interest deductions or the probability of experiencing losses) should only affect debt decisions to the extent that they affect a firm's marginal tax rate. Only for modestly profitable firms is it likely that nondebt tax shields have impact sufficient to affect the marginal tax rate and therefore debt policy.[13]

MacKie-Mason (1990) and Dhaliwal et al. (1992) address these issues by interacting NDTS with a variable that identifies firms near "tax exhaustion," at which point the substitution between nondebt tax shields and interest is most important. Both papers find that tax-exhausted firms substitute away from debt when nondebt tax shields are high.[14] Even though these papers find a negative relation between the interacted NDTS variable and debt usage, this solution is not ideal. For one thing, the definition of tax exhaustion is ad hoc. Moreover, Graham (1996a) shows that the interacted NDTS variable has low power to detect tax effects and that depreciation and investment tax credits (the traditional components of nondebt tax shields) have a very small empirical effect on the marginal tax rate. Ideally, researchers should capture the effects (if any) of nondebt tax shields, existing interest, and the probability of experiencing losses directly in the estimated

[13] The marginal tax rate for unprofitable firms will be close to zero whether or not the firm has NDTS. The tax rate for highly profitable firms will be near the top statutory rate, unless a firm has a very large amount of NDTS.

[14] Ekman (1995) finds the same for Swedish firms, as do Barthody and Mateus (2005) for Portuguese companies. Trezevant (1992) finds that Compustat PST firms most likely to be tax-exhausted decreased debt usage the most following the 1981 liberalization of tax laws that increased nondebt tax shields.

marginal tax rate, rather than including these factors as stand-alone variables.

A similar issue exists with respect to using profitability as a measure of tax status. Profitable firms usually have high tax rates and therefore some papers argue that the tax hypothesis implies they should use more debt. Empirically, however, the use of debt declines with profitability, which is often interpreted as evidence against the tax hypothesis (e.g., Myers, 1993). My view is that profitability should only affect the tax incentive to use debt to the extent that it affects the corporate marginal tax rate[15]; therefore, when testing for tax effects, the effects (if any) of profitability should be captured directly in the estimated MTR. Researchers would then interpret a stand-alone profitability variable as a control for potential nontax influences.

1.3.2 Directly estimating the marginal tax rate

One of the problems that led to Myers' capital structure puzzle is related to properly quantifying corporate tax rates and incentives. For example, many studies use static MTRs that ignore important dynamic features of the tax code related to net operating losses carryback and carryforwards, investment tax credits and other nondebt tax shields, and the alternative minimum tax. Static MTRs miss the fact that a company might be profitable today but expect to experience losses in the near future. This firm might erroneously be assigned a high current-period tax rate even though its true economic tax rate is low.[16] Conversely, an unprofitable firm might have a large current economic marginal tax rate if it is expected to soon become and remain profitable (because extra income earned today increases taxes paid in the future: an extra dollar of income today reduces losses that could be carried forward to delay future tax payments, thereby increasing present value tax liabilities).

[15] Keep in mind that a marginal tax rate is bound between zero and the top statutory rate while profitability is not bounded, which can introduce difficulties into interpreting profitability as a proxy for the tax rate.

[16] Scholes and Wolfson (1992) define the *economic marginal tax rate* as the present value of current and future taxes owed on an extra dollar of income earned today, which accounts for the probability that taxes paid today will be refunded in the near future.

Shevlin (1987, 1990) uses simulation techniques to capture the dynamic features of the tax code related to net operating loss carrybacks and carryforwards.[17] The first step in simulating an MTR for a given firm-year involves calculating the historic mean and variance of the change in taxable income for each firm. The second step uses this historic information to forecast future income for each firm. These forecasts can be generated with random draws from a normal distribution, with mean and variance equal to that gathered in the first step; therefore, many different forecasts of the future can be generated for each firm. The third step calculates the present value tax liability along each of the income paths generated in the second step, accounting for the tax-loss carryback and carryforward features of the tax code. The fourth step adds $1 to current year income and recalculates the present value tax liability along each path. The incremental tax liability calculated in the fourth step, minus that calculated in the third step, is the present value tax liability from earning an extra dollar today; in other words, the economic MTR. A separate marginal tax rate is calculated along each of the forecasted income paths to capture the different tax situations a firm might experience in different future scenarios. The idea is to mimic the different planning scenarios that a manager might consider. The fifth step averages across the MTRs from the different scenarios to calculate the expected economic marginal tax rate for a given firm-year. Note that these five steps produce the expected marginal tax rate for a single firm-year. The steps are replicated for each firm for each year, to produce a panel of firm-year MTRs. The marginal tax rates in this panel vary across firms and can also vary through time for a given firm. The end result is greater cross-sectional variation in corporate tax rates (and hence tax incentives) than implied by statutory rates.

One difficulty with simulated tax rates is that they require a time-series of firm-specific data. A second difficulty is that simulated tax rates are usually calculated using financial statement data, even though it would be preferable to use tax return data. Graham and Mills (2006)

[17] Auerbach and Poterba (1987) and Altshuler and Auerbach (1990) simulate tax rates using first-order Markov probabilities that weight the probability of transition between taxable and nontaxable states.

address both these problems by comparing several financial statement tax rates to simulated tax return tax rates. They find that the simulated financial statement tax rates are the best proxy for tax return tax rates, followed by a financial statement-based statutory tax rate.[18]

Note that by construction the simulated tax rates capture the influence of profitability on the corporate marginal tax rate. Graham (1996a) extends the simulation approach to directly capture the effects of nondebt tax shields, investment tax credits, and the alternative minimum tax. Using the simulated corporate marginal tax rates, Graham (1996a) documents a positive relation between tax rates and changes in debt ratios (consistent with Prediction 2), as do Graham et al. (1998) and Graham (1999) for debt levels. Since that time, numerous other studies have also used simulated tax rates to document tax effects in corporate financial decisions. These results help to resolve Myers' (1984) capital structure puzzle; when tax rates are properly measured, it is possible to link tax status with corporate debt policy.

1.3.3 Endogeneity of corporate tax status

Even if measured with a very precise technique, tax rates are endogenous to debt policy, which can have important effects on tax research. If a company issues debt, it reduces taxable income, which in turn can reduce its tax rate. The more debt issued, the greater the reduction in the marginal tax rate. Therefore, if one regresses debt ratios on marginal tax rates, the endogeneity of corporate tax status can impose a negative bias on the tax coefficient. This could explain the negative tax coefficient detected in some specifications (e.g., Hovakimian et al., 2001 and Barclay and Smith, 1995b). Note that endogeneity can affect

[18] Previous research by Graham (1996b) shows that an easy-to-calculate trichotomous variable (equal to the top statutory rate if a firm has neither negative taxable income nor NOL carryforwards, equal to one-half the statutory rate if it has one but not the other, and equal to zero if it has both) is a reasonable replacement for the simulated rate. Plesko (2003) compares financial-statement-based simulated rates for 586 firms to a static tax variable calculated using actual tax return data. He finds that simulated rates (based on financial statements) are highly correlated with tax variables based on tax return data. Plesko's evidence implies that the simulated tax rates are a robust measure of corporate tax status. Graham (1996b) suffers from the first difficulty mentioned in the text, Plesko by the second.

all sorts of tax variables, including those based on NOLs or that use an average tax rate (i.e., taxes paid/taxable income).

There are two solutions to the endogeneity problem. MacKie-Mason (1990) proposed the first solution by looking at (0,1) debt versus equity issuance decisions (rather than the debt level) in his influential examination of 1,747 issuances from 1977–1987. Debt levels (such as debt ratios) are the culmination of many historical decisions, which may obscure whether taxes influence current-period financing choice. Detecting tax effects in the incremental approach only requires that a firm make the appropriate debt-equity choice at the time of security issuance, given its current position, and not necessarily that the firm rebalance to its optimal debt-equity ratio with each issuance (as is implicit in many debt level studies). To avoid the endogenous effect of debt decisions on the marginal tax rate, MacKie-Mason uses the lagged marginal tax rate to explain current-period financing choice.[19] He finds a positive relation between debt issuance and tax rates. Graham (1996a) follows a similar approach and examines the relation between changes in the debt ratio and lagged simulated MTRs. He finds positive tax effects for a large sample of Compustat firms.[20]

If taxes exert a positive influence on each incremental financing decision, then the sum of these incremental decisions should show up in an analysis of current debt levels – if one could fix the endogenous negative effect on tax rates induced by cumulative debt usage.[21] The second

[19] Wang (2000) argues that firms do not consider the level of the marginal tax rate when making incremental decisions but rather consider how far the marginal tax rate is from the "optimal MTR." Holding the level of the tax rate constant, Wang shows that companies with tax rates above the optimum are those that use the most debt (an action which should endogenously reduce the marginal tax rate and move it closer to the optimum, essentially reducing MB until it equals MC). The difficulty with this approach is that Wang's "optimal MTR" is ad hoc and based on the probability of bankruptcy (as measured by Altman's Z-score).

[20] A number of other papers corroborate these results. For example, Shum (1996) finds similar evidence for Canadian firms. Alworth and Arachi (2000) show that lagged after-financing simulated tax rates are positively related to changes in debt for Italian firms. Henderson (2001) finds that changes in total liabilities and changes in long-term debt are both positively related to simulated tax rates in a sample of U.S. banks. Schulman et al. (1996) find that debt levels are positively correlated to tax rates in Canada and New Zealand.

[21] Dittmar (2002) studies corporate spin-offs, which potentially allows her to avoid the endogeneity problem by observing capital structures that are not the end result of a

approach to fixing the endogeneity problem is to measure tax rates "but for" financing decisions. Graham et al. (1998) measure tax rates before financing (i.e., based on income before interest is deducted). They find a positive relation between debt-to-value and (endogeneity-corrected) but-for tax rates. (They also find a "spurious" negative correlation in an experiment that uses an endogenously affected after-financing tax rate.)

Examining changes in debt answers the question "are incremental decisions affected by tax status?" An alternative approach is to ask "if tax rates exogenously change, how will a firm alter debt usage?" The Tax Reform Act of 1986 greatly reduced corporate marginal tax rates (see Fig. 1), which in isolation implies a reduction in the corporate use of debt. Givoly et al. (1992) find that firms with high tax rates prior to tax reform (firms that therefore probably experienced the largest drop in their tax rate) reduce debt the most after tax reform. This finding is somewhat surprising because their corporate marginal tax rate suffers from the negative endogeneity bias described above. Moreover, personal taxes are not modeled directly, even though they fell by more than corporate tax rates after the 1986 tax reform.[22] In a paper that examines international evidence during the same time period, Rajan and Zingales (1995) provide weak international evidence that taxes affect debt decisions.

1.3.4 Time-series and small firm evidence of tax effects

The empirical evidence described thus far confirms cross-sectionally that firms with high tax rates use more debt than those with low tax rates. Presumably, there should also be time-series tax effects. For example, if a firm starts public life with a low tax rate, one would expect increased debt usage if the tax rate increases as the firm matures. I am not aware of any study that documents tax-related time-series effects in debt usage. For example, Graham (1999) uses panel data to document

long history of accumulated debt policy decisions. However, it is still the case that past decisions can influence the parent's and/or spun-off unit's new capital structure. Dittmar does not find evidence that corporate tax rates affect spin-off debt ratios.

[22] Givoly et al. (1992) include lagged dividend yield in their specification to control for personal tax effects, which might allow their tax variable to isolate corporate tax effects. Personal tax effects are examined more fully in Section 1.4.

that cross-sectional variation in tax status affects debt usage but he finds no evidence that time-series variation does.

By studying capital structure decisions among newly formed firms, one might be able to avoid long-lasting effects of past financing decisions. For example, Baker and Wurgler (2002) show that today's market-to-book ratio and debt-equity issuance decisions continue to affect firm's debt ratios for ten or more years. Esty et al. (2000) describe various start-up financing issues including selecting a target debt ratio, as well as how market conditions and collateralization affect the sequence of initial financing choices.

Lemmon et al. (2006) show that firms retain close to their original debt ratios decades after first going public, even as tax status changes. Pittman and Klassen (2001) examine capital structure in the years following IPO. They perform annual (i.e., years since IPO) cross-sectional regressions and find evidence that taxes have a positive effect on the use of debt in the early years of a firm's public life – but this relation wanes as the firm ages. Pittman and Klassen attribute this waning to an increase in refinancing transactions costs as firms age. Note that their evidence is not time-series in terms of firms altering capital structure as tax rates change through time, though they do link debt policy to firm age. Pittman and Klassen also find that firms use relatively more NDTS as they age.

Almost all capital structure papers study Compustat companies. Ayers et al. (2001) instead examine small companies with less than 500 employees that participated in the 1993 Federal Reserve National Survey of Small Business Finances. 2,600 firms meet the Ayers et al. data requirements. The authors regress interest expense divided by pre-interest pre-NDTS income on various variables including tax expense divided by pre-interest income. They find a positive coefficient on the tax variable in both their outside and inside debt regressions (i.e., interest owed to non-owners and owners, respectively). It is difficult to compare their results to Compusat-based research because Ayers et al. use a different dependent variable than most studies, and they delete firms with a negative value for the dependent variable (which raises statistical issues).

To summarize Section 1.3, once issues related to measuring debt policy and tax rates are addressed, researchers have supplied evidence in response to Myers' (1984) challenge to show that corporate debt usage is positively affected by tax rates. These results are consistent with survey evidence that interest tax deductibility is an important factor affecting debt policy decisions (ranking below only maintaining financial flexibility, credit ratings, and earnings volatility), and is especially important for large industrial firms (Graham and Harvey, 2001). Notwithstanding these empirical results, Myers is still not entirely convinced (Myers et al., 1998); he argues that tax incentives are of "third order" importance in the hierarchy of corporate decisions. It would be helpful for future research to investigate whether the tax effects on debt versus equity choice are economically important, and if they are not, determine why not.

Several other challenges remain. First, none of the papers cited above provide time-series evidence that firm-specific changes in tax status affect debt policy. It would be quite helpful to examine whether a firm changes its debt policy as it matures and presumably its tax status changes. Second, Fama and French (2001) point out that with few exceptions the panel data examinations do not use statistical techniques that account for cross-correlation in residuals, and therefore many papers do not allow for proper determination of statistical significance for the tax coefficients. Therefore, it is not clear if all of the tax effects documented above are robustly significant. Finally, most papers ignore the tax cost of receiving interest income from the investor's perspective, an issue to which I now turn.

1.4 Empirical evidence on whether personal taxes affect corporate debt vs. equity policy

Miller (1977) identifies a puzzle: the benefits of debt seem large relative to expected costs, and yet many firms do not use much debt. Miller proposes that the personal tax cost of interest income (relative to the personal tax cost of equity) is large enough at the margin to completely offset the corporate tax advantage of debt. The Miller Equilibrium is difficult to test empirically for several reasons, not the least of which is that the identity and tax-status of the marginal investor(s) between debt and equity are unknown. Anecdotally, we can note that the tax rate on interest income (τ_P) was large relative to tax rates on corporate and equity income (τ_C and τ_E) when Miller wrote his paper, so the Miller Equilibrium was plausible. However, the statutory tax rates shown in Fig.1 imply that expression (1) has been positive since 1981, so the strict form of the Miller Equilibrium is less plausible in the last two decades.[23]

From the corporate perspective, the relatively high investor-level taxation of interest leads to a "personal tax penalty" for debt: investors demand a higher risk-adjusted return on debt than on equity. By rearranging Equation (1.1), the net tax advantage of debt can be represented as

$$\tau_C - [\tau_P - (1 - \tau_C)\tau_E], \tag{1.6}$$

where τ_C is the corporate income tax rate, τ_E is the personal tax rate on equity income, and τ_P is the personal tax rate on interest income. The bracketed term in Eq. (1.6) accounts for the personal tax penalty: $\tau_P - (1 - \tau_C)\tau_E$.

To quantify the effect of personal taxes in expression (5), Gordon and MacKie-Mason (1990) and others implicitly assume that investors form clienteles based on firm-specific dividend payout ratios, and therefore that τ_E is a weighted combination of the tax rates on dividend payout and capital gains income: $\tau_E = (payout)\tau_{div} + (1 - payout)\tau_{\text{cap gains}}$. This and related papers use historic averages to estimate dividend payout and measure τ_{div} as equaling τ_P, where τ_P is implicitly estimated using the difference between the yield on taxable and tax-free government bonds. $\tau_{\text{cap gains}}$ is often assumed to equal a fraction of the statutory capital gains tax rate (to capture the benefit of reduced effective tax rates due to deferral of equity taxation and omission of equity tax at death).[24]

---

[23] If the statutory tax rates depicted in Fig. 1 are not representative of the tax rates applicable to the marginal investor(s), or if capital gains tax rates are effectively reduced through deferral and/or elimination at death, then the Miller Equilibrium is technically possible even in recent years.

[24] Green and Hollifield (2003) simulate an economy to investigate the degree to which capital gains deferral reduces the effective tax rate on equity income (and therefore, from the company's perspective, increases the personal tax penalty for debt relative to equity). Green and Hollifield find that the ability to defer taxation reduces the implicit tax on capital gains by about 60%. If they were to factor in deferral at death and the lower

Given these assumptions, Gordon and MacKie-Mason (1990) estimate that the tax advantage of debt, net of the personal tax penalty, increased following the Tax Reform Act of 1986. Recall that Miller (1977) implies that the aggregate supply of debt is determined by relative corporate and personal tax rates. Gordon and MacKie-Mason document that aggregate corporate debt ratios increased slightly in response to tax reform (consistent with Prediction 4). This is the only research of which I am aware that investigates this aggregate prediction. Note that Gordon and MacKie-Mason focus on a single point in time, while the Miller Equilibrium has implications for any point in time. Also note that if the marginal investor is taxable at rates like those reflected in Fig. 1, then the 2003 reduction in dividend and capital gains tax rates to $\tau_{div} = \tau_P = 15\%$ should reduce the aggregate amount of debt used in the U.S. economy.

Graham (1999) tests similar predictions using firm-specific data. He finds that the net tax advantage of the first dollar of interest averaged between 140 and 650 basis points between 1980 and 1994.[25] He finds that the firms for which the net advantage is largest use the most debt in virtually every year. Graham also separately identifies a positive (negative) relation between the corporate tax rate (personal tax penalty) and debt usage. These results are consistent with Predictions 2 and 3. In contrast, while Dhaliwal et al. (2005) find evidence that interest deductibility reduces the cost of capital (consistent with Prediction 2),

tax rate on capital gains relative to the rate on dividends and interest, it would reduce the implicit tax rate on capital gains even further. (On the other hand, their calculations ignore the high turnover frequently observed for common stocks and mutual funds, which increases the effective tax rate on equity.) Overall, their evidence suggests that there is a measurable personal tax disadvantage to debt but it does not appear large enough to offset the corporate tax benefits of debt. However, Green and Hollifield find that when coupled with fairly small costs of bankruptcy (e.g., realized bankruptcy costs equal to 3% of pretax firm value), the personal tax penalty is sufficient to offset the corporate tax advantage to debt at the margin and lead to interior optimal debt ratios.

[25] I update Graham's (1999) annual tax regressions from his Table 5.1, Panel B. The tax variable is the tax advantage of debt net of personal taxes, as expressed in Eq. (1.5), with the personal tax penalty based on firm-specific dividend payout ratios. The dependent variable is debt-to-value. The estimated tax coefficients for 1995–1999 are 0.072, 0.046, 0.103, 0.135, 0.191, respectively, indicating that debt ratios are positively related to net tax incentives. All the tax coefficients are significant at a 1% level, except in 1996 when the p-value is 0.026.

they do not find evidence that personal taxes affect the cost of capital (lack of evidence relative to Prediction 3).

Campello (2001) assumes that a given firm's debt *and* equity are held by a particular clientele of investors (with the clienteles based on investor tax rates). He investigates the capital structure response to the large reduction in personal taxes (relative to the smaller reduction in corporate tax rates) after the Tax Reform Act of 1986. Campello finds that zero-dividend firms (which presumably have high-tax-rate investors and therefore experienced the largest reduction in the personal tax penalty) increased debt ratios in response to tax reform, while high-dividend payout firms (which presumably have low-tax-rate investors and therefore experienced a small reduction in the personal tax penalty) reduced debt usage relative to peer firms.

1.4.1 Market-based evidence on how personal taxes affect security returns

While consistent with personal taxes affecting corporate financing decisions in the manner suggested by Prediction 3, the papers cited above are not closely tied to market-based evidence about the tax characteristics of the marginal investor between debt and equity. Instead, these papers assume that dividend clienteles exist, and also make assumptions about the personal tax characteristics of these clienteles based on a firm's payout policy. For example, these papers implicitly assume that there is a certain marginal investor who owns both equity and debt *and* (to estimate τ_P) that this same investor sets prices between taxable and tax-free bonds. The truth is that we know very little about the identity or tax-status of the marginal investor(s) between any two sets of securities, and deducing this information is difficult.

For example, assume that munis yield 7%, Treasuries 10%, and equities 8% (and assume that this equity return has been adjusted to make its risk equivalent to the risk of munis and Treasuries). In a Gordon/MacKie-Mason/Graham type of equilibrium, $r_{\text{muni}} = r_{\text{Treasury}}(1 - \tau_P) = r_{\text{equity}}(1 - \tau_{\text{equity}}) = 7\%$, which implies that τ_P=30% and $\tau_{\text{equity}} = 12.5\%$. This in turn implies that a large portion of equity returns are expected to come from capital gains (because

τ_{equity} is so much lower than τ_P). However, things are rarely so simple. First, it is difficult to determine the risk-adjusted equity return.[26] Second, if there are frictions or transactions costs limiting arbitrage between pairs of markets (or if risk adjustments are not perfect), one could observe, say, munis yielding 7%, Treasuries 10%, and equities 12%. In this case, it is not clear which pair of securities should be used to deduce τ_P. If Treasuries and equities are used, the implicit τ_P could be negative. For example, assume that dividend payout is 15%, that $\tau_{\text{effective cap gains}} = 5\%$, and that τ_{equity} is modeled as a weighted average between dividends and retained earnings: $\tau_{\text{equity}} = 0.15(1 - \tau_{\text{div}}) + 0.85(1 - \tau_{\text{effective cap gains}})$, where $\tau_{\text{div}} = \tau_P$. To ensure that $r_{\text{Treasury}}(1 - \tau_P) = r_{\text{equity}}(1 - \tau_{\text{equity}})$, in this example $\tau_P = -30\%$; clearly, market frictions drive relative returns in this example, so the usual approach can not be used to deduce the personal tax characteristics of the marginal investor(s).

Williams (2000) points out that when there are more than two assets, different pairs of assets can be arbitraged by different investors, so prices might reflect a mixture of tax characteristics. It is difficult to know which assets are directly benchmarked to each other by the marginal investor(s) and which are "indirectly arbitraged," and it is even difficult to know whether capital gains or income tax rates are priced into security returns.

It would be helpful if future research could quantify the relative importance of personal taxes on security prices, with an eye towards feedback into capital structure decisions. One area where there has been a fair amount of research along these lines involves determining the investor tax rate implicit between municipals and taxable government bonds. Poterba (1989) finds that the yield difference between high-grade one-year munis and government bonds approximates the top statutory personal tax rate, implying that the marginal investor

[26] Gordon and MacKie-Mason (1990) and Graham (1999) avoid the issue of adjusting the equity return. Instead, they assume that τ_{div} equals the τ_P implicit between munis and Treasuries, that $\tau_{\text{effective cap gains}} = 0.25\text{x } \tau_{\text{statutory capital gains}}$, and weight these two pieces by the portion of earnings returned as dividends and retained, respectively, to deduce τ_{equity}. It would be informative if future research could calibrate this approach to market-driven estimates of τ_{equity}.

between these two securities is a highly taxed individual. However, even this experiment is not without difficulty. First, returns on long-term munis and taxables imply a tax rate for the marginal investor that is approximately half that implied by the short-term securities. Chalmers (1998) shows that this holds even when the muni interest payments are prefunded by T-bonds held in "defeasement," and therefore differences in risk between munis and T-bonds do not explain this conundrum. Green (1993) proposes that taxable bonds might not be "fully taxable" because a portion of their return can come from capital gains (especially for long-term bonds) and also because to some degree the interest income can be offset by investment interest deductions. Mankiw and Poterba (1996) suggest that munis might be benchmarked to equities by one clientele of investors and taxable bonds might be benchmarked to equities by another clientele. In this case, munis and taxables might not be directly benchmarked to each other, which could explain the unusual implicit tax rate that is sometimes observed between the two securities.

As an example of trying to link the effects of personal taxes to capital structure issues, consider the implications from Engel and Maydew (1999) and Irvine and Rosenfeld (2000) about the personal tax penalty.[27] Assume that corporations are the marginal investors in preferred stock but not in debt.[28] Given the similarity of the securities,

---

[27] Recall that these authors investigate MIPS for preferred exchanges. These two securities are similar in most respects, except that MIPS interest is tax deductible for issuing corporations and preferred dividends are not. On the investor side, corporate investors can take the 70% dividends received deduction (DRD) for preferred dividends but recipients of MIPS interest receive no parallel deduction.

[28] Erickson and Maydew (1998) provide evidence that corporations are the marginal investors in preferred stock, though they do not precisely identify the numeric value of the marginal investor's tax rate. They study the market reaction to the announced (but never implemented) change in the dividends received deduction (DRD). The DRD allows corporations to deduct a portion of the dividends they receive from other corporations to attenuate "triple taxation" of equity income. Individual investors do not receive the DRD. When the Treasury made a surprise announcement in December, 1995 that they were planning to reduce the deduction from 70% to 50%, the typical preferred stock experienced a statistically significant −1% abnormal return, while there was no reaction among common stocks. This implies that corporations are the marginal investors (i.e., price-setters) in preferred stocks but not in common stocks. One advantage of the Erickson and Maydew study is that they are able to control for risk when examining abnormal returns because they compare a security to itself before and after the exogenous

in equilibrium we expect their after-investor-tax returns to be equal, within transactions cost bounds: $r_{\text{preferred}}(1-\tau_{\text{DRD}}) = r_{\text{MIPS}}(1-\tau_P)$. Plugging in $r_{\text{preferred}} = 8.14\%$ and $r_{\text{MIPS}} = 8.37\%$ from Engel et al.'s Table 5.1, and assuming that the marginal corporate investor is taxed at 35% so that $\tau_{\text{DRD}} = 10.5\%$, we can back out the personal tax rate associated with interest income: $0.0814(1-0.105) = 0.0837(1-\tau_P)$ implies that $\tau_P = 13\%$. If I ignore the 30 basis point "yield premium" on MIPS imputed by Engel et al. and use $r_{\text{MIPS}} = 8.67\%$, $\tau_P = 16\%$.

To the extent that results based on MIPS interest carry over to debt interest, finding $\tau_P = 16\%$ for the marginal debt investor is intriguing. First note that the mean after-financing corporate tax rate in 1993–1999 is approximately 18% (see Table 1.1), which is a rough estimate of the tax benefit of the *last* dollar of interest deduction (ignoring all costs). If we make Miller's (1977) assumptions that $\tau_E = 0$ and that all firms face the same 18% marginal benefit of debt, then τ_P should equal 18% (i.e., MC should equal MB), quite close to the $\tau_P = 16\%$ MIPS estimate. As argued by Green and Hollifield (2003), it would only take fairly small costs of bankruptcy to equalize the costs and benefits of debt, creating an environment conducive to an equilibrium with internal optimal debt ratios. However, τ_E is most likely not zero for the marginal investor in equities. (Green and Hollifield argue that deferral reduces effective τ_E to about half its statutory level.) Another issue is that the estimated MIPS costs and benefits are average, not marginal. Even if the marginal costs and benefits are equal in an equilibrium like that depicted in Figure 1.1a, there is a firm surplus/benefit to using debt. Therefore, even if personal tax costs are large enough at the margin to equal marginal benefits, there appear to be tax-driven preferred

---

announcement. The authors are unable to precisely deduce the tax rate of the marginal (corporate) investor, however, because they can not pinpoint the probability assigned by the market that the Treasury would actually implement the proposal.

While Erickson and Maydew (1998) find no evidence that corporations are the marginal investors in common stocks, Geisler (1999) shows that common stock holdings by insurance companies vary positively with the allocation of the dividends received deduction among insurance companies. (The allocation of DRD can vary across insurance companies for regulatory reasons.) Geisler's evidence is consistent with clienteles: insurance companies respond to tax incentives to hold common stocks when their tax rate is low (i.e., when their DRD allocation is high).

capital structures for some firms – presumably the incremental benefit would be near \$0.35 per dollar for high-tax-rate firms, while the personal tax cost is only half that amount. Only if the nontax costs of debt are large for these high-tax rate firms could a Miller-type equilibrium hold, in which the benefits of debt are zero for all firms in equilibrium.

In sum, the implicit personal tax costs estimated here suggest that at the margin the tax costs and tax benefits might be of similar magnitude. However, they do not explain cross-sectionally why some inframarginal firms (with large tax benefits of interest) do not use more debt. More on this in Section 1.4. One other place where there has been a fair amount of success (though not unambiguously so) in deducing marginal investor tax characteristics is related to ex-day dividend returns. I defer this discussion to Section 3, where I explore how taxes affect corporate dividend policy.

In the most general sense, any research that shows that personal tax rates affect security returns sheds light on Miller's (1977) claims. Using the CAPM-with-taxes specification, Auerbach (1983) finds evidence that tax-related preferences result in clienteles of investors that purchase stocks based on firm-specific dividend-price ratios. Constantinides (1983) and Dammon et al. (2001) investigate how favorable capital gains taxation affects investment and consumption choices. Seida and Wempe (2000) show that individual investors accelerated recognizing capital gains (and delayed losses) in anticipation of the increase in capital gains tax rates associated with the 1986 tax act. See Poterba (2001) for a review of articles related to how personal taxation affects the timing and value of asset sales and purchases.

Tax capitalization Another group of papers investigates tax capitalization. These papers argue that personal taxes are capitalized into share prices via retained earnings. This in turn affects the relative tax advantage to debt because retained earnings are assumed to be the marginal source of funding. Harris and Kemsley (1999), Collins and Kemsley (2000), and related papers assume that all earnings are eventually paid out as taxable dividends (and none via repurchases or liquidating dividends), which is consistent with the "new view" of the effects of dividend taxation.[29] They argue that (nearly) full dividend taxation is impounded into share prices and therefore, there is no incremental personal tax penalty when a firm pays a dividend. Therefore, personal taxes are large on interest income and small on equity income, and the personal tax penalty to debt financing is large.

Harris and Kemsley (1999) regress stock price on variables including retained earnings, and they infer that retained earnings are penalized at a dividend tax rate of approximately 47%. Collins and Kemsley (2000) argue that reinvesting current earnings leads to investor capital gains taxation when shares are sold, on top of the already impounded dividend taxation. This implies that there is no personal tax penalty to dividend payments (it is already impounded into share prices and therefore paying a dividend does not lead to further valuation effects). In fact, this leads to the counterintuitive argument that paying dividends leads to a reduction in future capital gains payments and therefore, *dividend payments are tax advantageous.* This implication only holds if arbitrage by tax-free investors is restricted to the point that personal investors are the marginal price-setters in stocks. Collins and Kemsley find empirical evidence that they interpret as being consistent with their hypotheses. An untested implication of their argument is that there should be a large value gain in deals that result in firms returning capital to investors in any form other than taxable dividends (such as mergers). Research into this area could be informative.

Rather than dividend taxes, an alternative argument is that capital gains taxes on future earnings are impounded into share prices. Consider a shareholder in a nondividend-paying firm and assume that the firm is expected to pay dividends at some point in the distant future. If the market expects that low-tax investors are likely to be the dominant owners of this company when the dividend payments are initiated, the only (future) tax that current investors face is capital gains. In support of this argument, Lang and Shackelford (2000) show that upon announcement that capital gains tax rates were going to decline,

[29] See Auerbach (2002) for cites. The "new view" or "trapped equity" assumptions are in contrast to the assumptions I made at the beginning of Section 1 that "equity is the marginal source of funds" and that "dividends are paid out according to a fixed payout policy."

stock prices increased most among firms for which capital gains are most important (i.e., firms with the lowest dividend yield). This is opposite the reaction predicted by lock-in models like Klein (2001), in which returns fall when capital gains rates fall, for firms with substantial accrued retained earnings, because the required return declines along with the tax rate. Dai et al. (2006) find evidence of a capitalization effect after announcement that the Taxpayer Relief Act of 1997 would reduce capital gains tax rates, and evidence of a lock-in effect when the act became effective. See Shackelford and Shevlin (2001) for further discussion of the tax capitalization literature.

Overall, the tax status of the marginal investor and therefore the empirical magnitude of the personal tax penalty is an open empirical question. This is an important issue. For one thing, failing to control for personal tax considerations can result in an omitted variable bias. For example, personal tax considerations could cause clientele behavior that is correlated with dividend-payout ratios. In a regression that omits personal tax considerations, the dividend-payout coefficient might erroneously be interpreted as supporting a nontax hypothesis. As another example, business students are often taught that the tax advantage of debt is captured by τ_CD (see eq. (1.4)), which ignores personal tax effects. If it can be demonstrated that personal tax effects are not particularly important, this simplified view of the world might be justified. In contrast, if investor taxes affect security returns in important ways, more care needs to be taken in modeling these effects in corporate finance research. Investigations of personal tax effects face several challenges, not the least of which is that risk-differences between securities must be properly controlled to allow one to deduce implicit tax rates from market return data.

1.5 Beyond debt vs. equity

Leasing The discussion thus far has considered the debt versus equity choice; however, it can be extended to leasing arrangements. In certain circumstances, a high-tax rate firm can have a tax incentive to borrow to purchase an asset, even if it allows another firm to lease and use the asset. With true leases (as defined by the IRS) the lessor purchases an asset, and deducts depreciation and (if it borrows to buy) interest from taxable income. The lessee, in turn, obtains use of the asset but can not deduct interest or depreciation. The depreciation effect therefore encourages low-tax rate firms to lease assets from high-tax-rate lessors. This occurs because the lessee effectively "sells" the depreciation (and associated tax deduction) to the lessor, who values it more highly (assuming that the lessee has a lower tax rate than the lessor). This incentive for low-tax rate firms to lease is magnified when depreciation is accelerated, relative to straight line depreciation. Further, the alternative minimum tax (AMT) system can provide an additional incentive for a lessee to lease, in order to remove some depreciation from its books and stay out of AMT status altogether.

There are other tax effects that can reinforce or offset the incentive for low tax rate firms to lease. Lessors with relatively large tax rates receive a relatively large tax benefit of debt, which provides an additional incentive (to borrow to) buy an asset and lease it to the lessee. Moreover, tax incentives provided by investment tax credits (which have existed at various times but are not currently on the books in the U.S.) associated with asset purchsaes are also relatively beneficial to high tax-rate lessors. In contrast, the relatively high taxes that the lessor must pay on lease income provide a tax disincentive for firms with high tax rates to be lessors (and similarly the relatively small tax benefit that a low tax rate firm obtains from deducting lease expense works against the incentive for low tax rate firms to lease rather than buy). The traditional argument is that low tax rate firms have a tax incentive to lease from high tax rate lessors, though this implication is only true for some combinations of tax rules (e.g., depreciation rules, range of corporate tax rates, existence of investment tax credits or AMT) and leasing arrangements (e.g., structure of lease payments). See Smith and Wakeman (1985) for details on how nontax effects can also influence the leasing decision.

Prediction 5 All else equal, the traditional argument is that low tax-rate firms should lease assets from high-tax rate lessors, though this implication is conditional on specifics of the tax code and leasing contract.

There are several complications associated with investigating whether firms lease in response to tax incentives. First, because leasing expense is tax deductible, leasing endogenously reduces a lessee's effective tax rate, which can bias an experiment in favor of detecting tax effects. Likewise, lessor tax rates could be endogenously increased from the effects of lease income. Second, financial statement definitions of leasing are not one-to-one with IRS definitions, making it difficult to use Compustat data to test Prediction 5. Using endogenously-affected tax variables, Barclay and Smith (1995b) and Sharpe and Nguyen (1995) find that low-tax-rate firms use relatively many capital leases. However, capital leases do not meet the IRS definition of true leases (instead they are likely a mixture of true leases and conditional sales contracts, the latter of which are treated like debt so the lessee deducts interest and depreciation), and therefore the documented negative relation between capital leases and taxes is hard to interpret because it might be spurious.

Graham et al. (1998) address the first issue by measuring tax incentives "but-for financing decisions," i.e., calculating tax rates using income before debt interest and the implicit interest portion of lease payments are deducted. They address the second issue by focusing on operating leases, which are defined in a manner similar to the IRS definition of true leases. Graham et al. (1998) find that the use of operating leases is negatively related to before-financing tax rates, consistent with Prediction 5, and that capital leases are unrelated to before-financing tax rates. Graham et al. also show that erroneously using an after-financing tax rate would double the magnitude of the negative tax coefficient for operating leases, and spuriously assign a negative tax coefficient to capital lease usage.

Eades and Marston (2001) find that lessors tend to be high-tax rate firms (consistent with Prediction 5). Finally, O'Malley (1996) finds no evidence that firms systematically lease in response to tax incentives imposed by the AMT. We need research investigating whether the tax benefit of leasing adds to firm value. The jury is also still out on whether debt and leasing are substitutes for the lessee (as they might be in a DeAngelo and Masulis, 1980 sense because both lead to tax deductions).

Pensions Black (1980) assumes that pension plans and the overall company are a single economic entity that should have an integrated financing and investment strategy. Due to interest tax deductions, the cost of corporate borrowing is the after-tax cost of debt. Because they are tax-free entities, defined benefit pension plans (DBs) earn the before-tax rate of interest on bond holdings. Therefore, Black suggests that DBs should increase (decrease) bond (equity) holdings, while the rest of the firm should do the reverse. This action should not increase firm risk because the increase in corporate debt offerings is offset by the increase in bonds held in the pension plan. In a M&M (1963) world, the net effect is that the company earns τ_C times the amount of bonds held, as in Eq. (1.4). Tepper (1981) argues that there can be a tax advantage to the strategy of corporate borrowing and DBs investing in bonds, even in a Miller (1977) world. In this case, the benefit occurs when the DB is an inframarginal investor in bonds, thereby earning the "extra" return necessary to compensate individual investors for the personal tax penalty associated with interest income (i.e., DBs capture some of the investor surplus depicted in Figure 1.1). The Tepper incentive for DBs to hold bonds increases with the difference between personal tax rates on interest and equity income.

Prediction 6 Defined benefit pension plans have an incentive to hold bonds (equity) that increases (decreases) in the corporate tax rate, while the rest of the firm has the reverse incentive.

Frank (2002) finds evidence consistent with the Black (1980) case: she finds that DB bond holdings increase with a simulated corporate marginal tax rate. She does not find evidence consistent with the Tepper argument. In a less direct test of the same incentives, Thomas (1988) finds time-series evidence that firms decrease DB contributions when their tax rate is falling, and cross-sectional evidence that high-tax firms have larger DB funding levels.

Clinch and Shibano (1996) study pension reversions, which occur when a firm terminates an overfunded pension, settles its liabilities, and reverts the excess assets to the firm, all in one year. The reverted assets are taxable in the reversion year. Clinch and Shibano find that firms with the largest tax benefit of reverting do so, and also that firms time reversion decisions to occur in years with particularly large tax benefits. One nice thing about the Clinch and Shibano experiment is that their tax variable equals the tax consequence of reverting relative to the tax consequence associated with the next best alternative (e.g., amortizing the excess assets over several years).[30]

Stefanescu (2006) studies whether defined pension obligations, which are akin to off-balance sheet debt, displace the use of balance sheet debt along the lines of suggested in DeAngelo and Masulis (1980). Pension contributions to DB plans are tax deductible and therefore are a form of nondebt tax shield that might substitute for interest deductions (Section 1.1). Stefanescu finds that considering pension deductions increases the overall measure of the tax benefits of debt by nearly one half, and reduces the Graham (2000) kink measure of debt conservatism by nearly one-third. She also concludes that one dollar of pension obligation reduces debt on the balance sheet by $0.36.

Debt maturity In the spirit of Modigliani and Miller (1985), Lewis (1990) derives an irrelevance null hypothesis for debt maturity. If corporate taxes are the only market imperfection, Lewis shows that the optimal firm-specific debt policy (i.e., optimal level of promised interest payments) can be achieved by various combinations of short- and long-term debt. This implies that firm value is unaffected by debt maturity structure and that capital market imperfections beyond corporate taxes, like costs to restructuring debt or underinvestment, are needed for debt maturity to matter.

Rather than modeling the simultaneous choice of debt level and maturity structure as in Lewis (1990), Brick and Ravid (1985) assume

[30] Chaplinsky and Niehaus (1990) describe the potential tax benefits of Employee Stock Ownership Plans, a form of defined contribution benefit plan. ESOPs offer deferred compensation to employees and a deductible expense to employers. ESOPs are designed to allow firms to borrow to purchase own-company stock on employees' behalf, which provides an interest deduction to the firm. Moreover, half of the interest income received by the lenders is tax-free. Shackelford (1991) finds that lenders keep only 20–30% of the tax benefit associated with this interest, with the remainder being passed along to the ESOP in the form of a lower interest rate on the loan. In late 1989, tax rules changed to restrict the interest exclusion to loans where the ESOP own more than 50% of the stock, which effectively killed the interest exclusion except for a few very unusual cases.

that firms choose debt level before debt maturity. If the expectations theory of interest rates holds, firms pay the same present value of interest in the long run regardless of debt maturity; however, issuing long-term debt accelerates interest payments, thus maximizing the present value of the interest tax shield. Brick and Ravid (1985) use this logic to argue that debt maturity should increase with the slope in the yield curve.

Prediction 7 Debt maturity increases in the slope of the yield curve.

Most empirical evidence does not support this prediction. Barclay and Smith (1995a) and Stohs and Mauer (1996) include a stand-alone yield curve variable that is either insignificant or has the wrong sign. Guedes and Opler (1996) argue that the slope of the yield curve should only affect firms with a positive tax rate, and therefore interact the yield curve variable with the corporate marginal tax rate. Neither Guedes and Opler (using a crude measure of the corporate tax rate), nor Harwood and Manzon (2000, using a simulated corporate tax rate) find a significant coefficient on the yield curve variable. The one exception is Newberry and Novack (1999), who use a dummy variable equal to one during 1992 and 1993 (when the term premium was relatively high) and equal to zero for all other years 1987–1995. Newberry and Novack find a positive coefficient on the yield curve dummy in their public debt regression but not in their private debt analysis.

Kane et al. (1985) determine optimal debt maturity in a model that trades off corporate tax benefits with personal tax, bankruptcy, and flotation costs. The implications of their model are that debt maturity decreases with the corporate MTR and increases with the personal tax rate: long maturity implies less frequent recapitalization and relatively low transactions costs, so long-term debt can be desireable even if the net tax benefit is low. Maturity also decreases with the volatility of firm value because volatile firms are more likely to restructure debt.

Prediction 8 Debt maturity decreases with the corporate MTR and the volatility of firm value and increases with the personal tax rate.

Stohs and Mauer (1996) find support for the latter prediction: volatile firms generally use shorter term debt. The evidence is weaker related to the tax rate prediction. Stohs and Mauer find that debt maturity decreases with corporate tax rates – but their MTR variable is very crude (equal to income tax expense divided by pretax income when this ratio is between zero and one, and equal to zero otherwise). Guedes and Opler (1996) find a negative coefficient on a tax expense divided by assets variable but the wrong sign on an NOL-based tax variable. Finally, Harwood and Manzon (2000) and Newberry and Novack (1999) find a positive relation between a simulated tax variable and debt maturity, opposite the Kane et al. prediction.[31] A positive coefficient makes sense if large simulated MTRs identify firms that use long-term debt cause they are relatively likely to be able to deduct interest in current and future periods.

Finally, debt maturity can affect the tax-timing option for firms to opportunely retire debt (e.g., Emery et al., 1988). If the corporate tax function is convex, the expected present value tax benefit of short-term debt declines with interest rate volatility, while the tax deductions with long-term debt are fixed. Therefore, long-term debt is preferred when interest rates are volatile. Long-term debt also increases the value of the timing option for investors to tax-trade securities (Kim et al., 1995) because option value increases with security maturity and long-term bond prices are more sensitive to changes in interest rates.

Prediction 9 Debt maturity increases with interest rate volatility.

Kim et al. (1995) find that debt maturity increases with interest rate volatility but Guedes and Opler (1996) do not. Nor do Guedes

[31] Harwood and Manzon's variable equals the Graham (1996a) simulated tax rate divided by the top statutory tax rate. This variable has a large value for firms that do not currently have NOLs and that do not expect to experience a loss in the near future. Harwood and Manzon predict a positive relation between this tax variable and debt maturity. They argue that firms with large values for the tax variable are likely to fully utilize tax deductions in the future, and therefore lock into long-term debt now. In new analysis for this chapter, I perform a more direct test on the hypothesis that uncertainty about future tax-paying status reduces the use of long-term debt. I use the standard deviation of the simulated marginal tax rate to measure uncertainty about tax-paying status, with the standard deviation calculated across the simulated scenarios for any given firm-year. I do not find any relation between debt maturity and uncertainty about tax-paying status.

and Opler find significance for a second variable that interacts interest rate volatility with a corporate MTR variable.

The evidence linking tax incentives to debt maturity is mixed. One thing that makes it difficult to draw general conclusions is that debt maturity is defined differently in various papers. Barclay and Smith (1995a) use a dependent variable measuring the portion of outstanding debt that matures in four or more years, Guedes and Opler (1996) use the log of the term to maturity for new debt issues, Stohs and Mauer (1996) use the book value weighted-average of the maturity of a firm's outstanding debt, Newberry and Novack use the same for new issues, and Harwood and Manzon (2000) use the portion of outstanding debt that is long-term. Another issue that might affect inference about tax variables is the apparently nonlinear relation between debt maturity and nontax influences (Guedes and Opler, 1996). Unless the nonlinearity of the overall specification is properly controlled, it might adversely affect the ability to detect tax effects. Finally, the yield curve was never inverted during the periods studied by most of these papers, so the tests of Brick and Ravid (1985) focus on the steepness of the yield curve, rather than the sign.

2

Taxes and Capital Structure – International Tax Issues

Section 1 reviews capital structure in the context of a domestic-only firm operating in a classical tax system (in which interest is tax deductible but equity payments are not). While much academic research focuses on this paradigm, international tax issues are becoming increasingly important. This section reviews how international tax law can affect corporate financing decisions in a multinational firm. The perspective is generally for a firm headquartered in the U.S. but many of the implications hold if the firm is headquartered elsewhere.

The general framework is still based on taxes affecting firm value via an expression like $V_{\text{with debt}} = V_{\text{no debt}} + \tau_C(.)\text{*D}$. The research in this section demonstrates that multinational tax rules can affect the $\tau_C(.)$ function and therefore the incentive to use both domestic and foreign debt. So as not to bog down in international tax law, this section only sketches the effects of multinational tax incentives. To focus on the central factors that affect multinational firms, I make several simplifying assumptions (described below). For a more detailed description of international tax law, see Hines (1996) or Scholes et al. (2002) and the references therein.

2.1 Tax incentives and financial policy in multinational firms: Theory and tax rules

A multinational corporation can finance its foreign operations with internal equity (i.e., an equity infusion from a parent or subsidiary to an affiliated subsidiary), internal debt (i.e., a loan from the parent to a subsidiary), external funding, or earnings retained by the foreign subsidiary. If internal equity is used, the parent receives its return on equity when the subsidiary repatriates dividends back to the home country. Dividend repatriations based on active operating earnings can usually be deferred indefinitely, until the parent needs an infusion of cash, or to optimize the worldwide tax situation of the firm.[1] In contrast, interest from internal debt is paid according to a fixed schedule. Like a repatriated dividend, interest counts as "world-wide income" on the U.S. tax return of the parent. Unlike a repatriated dividend, the interest is often deductible on the foreign tax return, allowing for a foreign tax deduction analogous to the tax benefit of debt described in Section 1.[2]

Two important items affect the financing choices of U.S.-based multinational firms: foreign tax credits and interest allocation rules. The U.S. government taxes individuals and corporations on the basis of residence or place of incorporation, meaning that they are taxed because they are from the U.S., regardless of where they earn income. (Note that the U.S. only taxes foreign source income at the time of repatriation to the U.S. parent.) At the same time, the government recognizes that income earned abroad is usually taxed by a foreign government, so the U.S. offers foreign tax credits to offset taxes paid abroad. If the U.S. did not offer such credits, the foreign operations

[1] To illustrate the potential economic importance of repatriations and taxes on such transfers, the 2003 tax bill included a one year window that allowed repatriation at a tax rate of about 5%. The goal was to spur a return of capital to U.S. domiciled firms in hopes that these firms would productively invest the funds and stimulate the U.S. economy and create domestic jobs.

[2] There are restrictions to shifting interest deductions abroad by lending from the domestic parent to the foreign subsidiary: thin capitalization rules (i.e., limits on the magnitude of foreign debt ratios), withholding taxes imposed by the foreign government on interest payments and other repatriations, and netting rules that restrict the effect of interest payments on the determination of foreign source income (Newberry and Dhaliwal, 2001 and Scholes et al., 2002). For example, withholding taxes are above and beyond foreign income taxes and are collected by foreign governments on remittances to parent firms.

of U.S. corporations would face double taxation and therefore have a tough time competing with foreign corporations. For the purposes of this analysis, think of the foreign tax rate (τ_{For}) as a weighted average of tax rates the firm pays in the various countries in which it earns foreign income, with the weights being the relative share of active (i.e., non-passive) foreign source income repatriated from a particular country.

In simplest terms, if the foreign tax rate is smaller than the U.S. corporate income tax rate (τ_{US}), a firm receives credit for foreign taxes paid but still must remit to the U.S. government taxes equal to ($\tau_{\mathrm{US}} - \tau_{\mathrm{For}}$)*(foreign source income). Such a firm is called *deficit credit* because it lacks sufficient foreign tax credits (FTCs) to avoid all U.S. taxes. For example, if repatriated foreign earnings are \$200, $\tau_{\mathrm{For}} = 15\%$, and $\tau_{\mathrm{US}} = 35\%$, the firm must pay \$40 in tax to the U.S.

In contrast, if $\tau_{\mathrm{For}} > \tau_{\mathrm{US}}$, the firm does not have to pay U.S. tax because it receives foreign tax credits proportional to τ_{For}. For example, if $\tau_{\mathrm{For}} = 45\%$ and $\tau_{\mathrm{US}} = 35\%$ and repatriated earnings are \$200, the firm pays \$90 in foreign tax; however, the firm's foreign tax credits are limited to $\mathrm{FTC_{allow}} = \$70$ ($= \min[\$200\tau_{\mathrm{US}}, \$200\tau_{\mathrm{For}}]$), which is just enough to shield it from U.S. tax obligation. The \$20 in unused FTCs can be carried back up to two years or carried forward up to five years to offset taxes on repatriated income (or they can be deducted rather than used as a credit). This firm is *excess credit* because it has more FTCs than it is allowed to use in the current year and accumulates the excess tax credits to potentially shield income in another year. The tax benefit of debt, $\tau_C(.)$, can be modeled as a decreasing function of accumulated FTCs because FTCs can act as nondebt tax shields that are substituted for interest deductions.[3]

[3] FTCs can affect tax incentives to use debt in a manner that is not reflected in a one-period model. Assume that a multinational firm has accumulated unused FTCs that it has carried forward to the present (or assume that it anticipates receiving excess FTCs sometime in the next two years). If a firm has carried forward FTCs from previous years it very likely was excess credit, and therefore subject to $\tau_{\mathrm{For}} > \tau_{\mathrm{US}}$ at some point in the past. For the most part, a firm can use these accumulated FTCs only if the foreign tax rate becomes smaller than the U.S. corporate income tax rate. This can occur if there is an exogenous shift in relative tax rates (τ_{For} and τ_{US}) or if a firm repatriates more foreign source income from low-tax countries, thereby endogenously reducing the average τ_{For}. If a firm expects to use accumulated FTCs to reduce taxes, the FTCs compete with interest deductions in a DeAngelo-and-Masulis sense and reduce the incentive to finance with debt.

Prediction 10 All else equal, the incentive $\tau_C(.)$ to finance with domestic debt decreases with accumulated foreign tax credits for deficit credit firms.[4]

Prediction 10 is a static prediction. Considering the dynamic carryback and carryforward features of the tax code, a dynamic prediction is that the tax incentive to finance with debt decreases with the probability of a firm being deficit credit and the probability of accumulating FTCs.

The second important tax principle affecting multinational corporate financing decisions is the allocation of debt interest between domestic and foreign operations. Via the allocation of domestic interest, the U.S. limits allowable foreign tax credits, thereby possibly reducing the tax benefit of domestic debt. (The U.S. does this to limit tax deductions on debt that might possibly be used to finance foreign operations and produce foreign profits.) To implement this policy, the U.S. allocates domestic interest to foreign operations based on the proportion of total assets that are in foreign subsidiaries. In rough terms, if two-thirds of a company's worldwide assets are held by foreign subsidiaries, then two-thirds of domestic interest deductions are allocated to foreign income when determining the allowable-FTC calculation. Note that this is a U.S. government ruling and does not mean that foreign governments recognize the allocated interest as a deduction against foreign income. Also note that the allocation of a portion of domestic interest abroad technically affects only the allowable-FTC calculation; that is, ignoring FTC, domestic interest deductions are not directly affected.

[4] Consider a firm with \$1 in pre-tax foreign earnings that it will repatriate back to the U.S. to pay investors. Assume that the firm has \$0.15 in accumulated FTCs, $\tau_P = 0.40$, $\tau_E = 0.20$, $\tau_{\text{For}} = 0.20$, and the U.S. corporate tax rate is $\tau_{\text{US}} = 0.35$. Ignoring foreign considerations, $\tau_C = 0.35$ and eq. (1.1) equals 0.08, so it appears that the firm should finance with domestic debt. However, $\tau_C = 0.20$ once the effect of FTCs is considered (the firm pays \$0.20 in foreign tax and no U.S. tax because the accumulated FTCs offset any potential tax owed to the U.S.); therefore, eq. (1.1) equals –0.04 and the firm should finance with equity. This implication holds for deficit credit firms but not for excess credit firms (because an excess credit firm would not pay U.S. tax at repatriation, regardless of whether they have accumulated FTCs).

The interest allocation procedure can reduce the tax incentive for U.S. firms to use domestic debt because $\tau_C(.)$ also declines with the degree of interest allocation. When a firm is excess credit (i.e., $\tau_{\mathrm{US}} < \tau_{\mathrm{For}}$) and taxable on both foreign and domestic operations, the interest allocation procedure reduces the tax benefit of domestic interest deductions by setting $\tau_C(.)$ equal to $\tau_{\mathrm{US}}(.)$*[domestic assets/worldwide assets]. Thus, for excess credit firms the incentive to finance with domestic debt decreases with the proportion of assets held abroad.[5] One implication of the interest allocation rules is that debt policy research can not assume that financial statement (or Compustat) "domestic interest expense" is fully beneficial to U.S. multinationals.

Table 2.1 summarizes the tax incentives to use external domestic or foreign debt in a one-period model. The table is intended to be self-explanatory so I emphasize only the main points in the text. The model ignores personal taxes, carryforwards and carrybacks, and assumes that all foreign income is repatriated each year. The worldwide tax liability ($\mathrm{Tax}_{\mathrm{World}}$) is equal to the sum of U.S. tax on worldwide income ($\mathrm{Tax}_{\mathrm{US}}$) and foreign tax on foreign income ($\mathrm{Tax}_{\mathrm{For}}$), less allowable FTCs. The table shows the change in $\mathrm{Tax}_{\mathrm{World}}$ that occurs, for various tax credit and interest allocation situations, when an additional dollar of domestic or foreign interest is deducted.[6]

For the most part, the results in Table 2.1 are what you would expect without thinking too deeply about the complexities of foreign taxes. If $\mathrm{Tax}_{\mathrm{US}}$ is zero (rows (1) and (3)) or domestic income is negative (row (6)), there is no tax benefit from issuing domestic debt; there is, however, a benefit of τ_{For} to deducting \$1 of foreign interest when foreign income is positive (rows (1) and (6)).[7] If foreign income is negative but

[5] If a U.S. multinational is deficit credit (i.e., $\tau_{\mathrm{US}} > \tau_{\mathrm{For}}$) and taxable both in the U.S. and overseas, $\tau_C(.) = \tau_{\mathrm{US}}$ and the incentive to use domestic debt is not affected by interest allocation rules. The interest allocation rules limit the amount of deductions a firm is allowed to use to offset repatriated foreign income. When a firm is deficit credit, it pays tax at the rate τ_{US} regardless of the amount of FTCs applied to foreign-source income, so reducing allowable FTCs via interest allocation does not affect the current-year tax liability or tax incentives to use domestic debt.

[6] This model ignores many techniques by which firms can minimize worldwide taxes. See Scholes et al. (2002) for more information on these alternative mechanisms.

[7] If there is a positive probability that tax-losses will be used if carried backward or forward, the tax benefit can be positive even in rows (1), (3), or (6). Conversely, if there is a positive

Table 2.1 Tax incentive to use debt in a U.S. multinational firm with foreign tax credits and allocable domestic interest

Assume that a U.S. multinational firm currently returns \$1 of pre-corporate-tax earnings to its marginal investor as domestic equity. The one-period model in this table shows the tax effect of instead paying the \$1 as foreign interest (rightmost column in each panel below) or as \$1 of domestic interest (the second-to-rightmost column). The model is adapted from Collins and Shackelford (1992) and assumes that all foreign income ($\mathrm{Inc}_{\mathrm{For}}$) is repatriated every year and that tax rules are the same worldwide, except that only the U.S. allocates interest. The model ignores the AMT, carrybacks and carryforwards, personal taxes, and allocable items other than interest. Because the real-world tax-code is dynamic (i.e., allows for carrybacks and carryforwards), the one-period nature of this model might overstate (understate) the largest (smallest) tax benefits. Note that foreign losses (i.e., $\mathrm{Inc}_{\mathrm{For}} - \mathrm{Int}_{\mathrm{For}} < 0$) can not be repatriated as losses back to the U.S. $\mathrm{FTC}_{\mathrm{allow}}$ is allowable foreign tax credit (sometimes referred to as $\mathrm{FTC}_{\mathrm{limitation}}$), FA is foreign assets net of foreign debt, WA is worldwide assets net of foreign debt, and FSI is foreign source income, which equals $\mathrm{Inc}_{\mathrm{For}} - \mathrm{Int}_{\mathrm{For}} - \mathrm{Int}_{\mathrm{US}}$.

$\mathrm{Tax}_{\mathrm{World}} = \mathrm{Tax}_{\mathrm{US}} + \mathrm{Tax}_{\mathrm{For}} - \mathrm{FTC}_{\mathrm{allow}} = (\mathrm{Inc}_{\mathrm{US}} - \mathrm{Int}_{\mathrm{US}} + \mathrm{Inc}_{\mathrm{For}} - \mathrm{Int}_{\mathrm{For}})\tau_{\mathrm{US}} + (\mathrm{Inc}_{\mathrm{For}} - \mathrm{Int}_{\mathrm{For}})\tau_{\mathrm{For}} - \mathrm{FTC}_{\mathrm{allow}}$, where

$\mathrm{FTC}_{\mathrm{allow}} = \mathrm{Max}\{0, \mathrm{Min}[\mathrm{Tax}_{\mathrm{For}}, \mathrm{FSI}\tau_{\mathrm{US}}, \mathrm{Tax}_{\mathrm{US}}]\} = \mathrm{Max}\{0, \mathrm{Min}[(\mathrm{Inc}_{\mathrm{For}} - \mathrm{Int}_{\mathrm{For}})\tau_{\mathrm{For}}, (\mathrm{Inc}_{\mathrm{For}} - \mathrm{Int}_{\mathrm{For}} - \mathrm{Int}_{\mathrm{US}})\tau_{\mathrm{US}}, (\mathrm{Inc}_{\mathrm{US}} - \mathrm{Int}_{\mathrm{US}} + \mathrm{Inc}_{\mathrm{For}} - \mathrm{Int}_{\mathrm{For}})\tau_{\mathrm{US}}]\}$

	If $\mathrm{Tax}_{\mathrm{US}}$	and $\mathrm{Tax}_{\mathrm{For}}$	then $\mathrm{FTC}_{\mathrm{allow}} =$	and $\mathrm{Tax}_{\mathrm{World}} =$	$\delta(\mathrm{Tax}_{\mathrm{World}}/\delta(\mathrm{Int}_{\mathrm{US}})$	$\delta(\mathrm{Tax}_{\mathrm{World}})/\delta(\mathrm{Int}_{\mathrm{For}})$
(1)	$= 0$	> 0	0*	$(\mathrm{Inc}_{\mathrm{For}} - \mathrm{Int}_{\mathrm{For}})\tau_{\mathrm{For}}$	0	$-\tau_{\mathrm{For}}$
(2)	> 0	$= 0$	0	$(\mathrm{Inc}_{\mathrm{US}} - \mathrm{Int}_{\mathrm{US}})\tau_{\mathrm{US}}$	$-\tau_{\mathrm{US}}$	0
(3)	$= 0$	$= 0$	0	0	0	0

Otherwise, if $\text{Tax}_{\text{US}} > 0$ and $\text{Tax}_{\text{For}} > 0$ and

	if $\text{Inc}_{\text{US}} - \text{Int}_{\text{US}}$	and τ_{US}	then $\text{FTC}_{\text{allow}} =$	referred to as	$\delta(\text{Tax}_{\text{World}})/\delta(\text{Int}_{\text{US}})$	$\delta(\text{Tax}_{\text{World}})/\delta(\text{Int}_{\text{For}})$
(4)	> 0	$> \text{Tax}_{\text{For}}/\text{FSI}$	$(\text{Inc}_{\text{For}} - \text{Int}_{\text{For}})\tau_{\text{For}}$	deficit credit	$-\tau_{\text{US}}$	$-\tau_{\text{US}} - \tau_{\text{For}} + \tau_{\text{For}} = -\tau_{\text{US}}$
(5)	> 0	$< \tau_{\text{For}}$	$(\text{Inc}_{\text{For}} - \text{Int}_{\text{For}} - \frac{FA}{WA}\text{Int}_{\text{US}})\tau_{\text{US}}$	excess credit*	$-\tau_{\text{US}}\left(1 - \frac{FA}{WA}\right)$	$-\tau_{\text{US}} - \tau_{\text{For}} + \tau_{\text{US}} = -\tau_{\text{For}}$
(6)	< 0, and $< \text{Inc}_{\text{For}} - \text{Int}_{\text{For}}$ in absolute value, so some taxes paid	not applicable	$(\text{Inc}_{\text{US}} - \text{Int}_{\text{US}} + \text{Inc}_{\text{For}} - \text{Int}_{\text{For}})\tau_{\text{US}}$	domestic losses but worldwide profits (excess credit)*	0	$-\tau_{\text{US}} - \tau_{\text{For}} + \tau_{\text{US}} = -\tau_{\text{For}}$

*In a multi-period model, FTCs above the allowable amount could be carried back or accumulated and carried forward. For example, in the excess credit case with interest allocation (row (5)), $\frac{FA}{WA}$ of unused FTCs accumulate per incremental dollar of domestic interest.

domestic income is positive (row (2)), there is no tax incentive to issue foreign debt but an incremental dollar of domestic interest provides a benefit of τ_{US}.

Two situations are more subtle. If a U.S. multinational is deficit credit (i.e., τ_{US} is greater than τ_{For}) and profitable both in the U.S. and overseas (row (4)), a dollar of domestic or foreign interest produces a tax benefit of τ_{US}. To see how foreign interest produces a tax benefit proportional to τ_{US}, consider a case in which a multinational earns \$2 in a country with $\tau_{\text{For}} = 45\%$ and \$4 in a country with $\tau_{\text{For}} = 25\%$, and assume that $\tau_{\text{US}} = 35\%$. The \$2 of high-tax foreign income produces $\text{Tax}_{\text{For}} = \$0.90$. The firm receives $\text{FTC}_{allow} = \$0.70$ on this income and has \$0.20 of unused FTCs. The \$4 of low-tax foreign income produces $\text{Tax}_{\text{For}} = \$1.00$. As a stand-alone item, this income produces \$0.40 of U.S. tax at repatriation (\$4*(35%-25%)); however, the \$0.20 of extra FTC offsets half of this U.S. tax liability. On net the firm pays the U.S. \$0.20 in tax on repatriated foreign earnings and has a total tax liability of $\text{Tax}_{\text{World}} = \$2.10$ (\$2.10 = \$0.90 in high-tax country, \$1.00 in low-tax country, and \$0.20 on income repatriated from low-tax country).[8] If this firm deducts \$1 of interest in the low-tax country, it reduces its tax bill by \$0.35 (\$0.25 reduction in Tax_{For} and \$0.10 reduction in U.S. tax owed on that dollar). If the firm uses \$1 of interest in the high-tax country, it reduces its tax bill by \$0.35 (\$0.45 reduction in Tax_{For} but \$0.10 less FTC available to offset taxes owed on the income repatriated from the low-tax country.) Either way, the tax benefit of deducting \$1 of foreign interest is τ_{US} when a firm is deficit credit and profitable both in the U.S. and overseas.

The second subtle situation involves the tax benefit of deducting domestic interest when a firm is excess credit and Tax_{US} and Tax_{For}

probability that losses will occur and be carried back from the future, positive tax benefits might be smaller than those shown in the table. Also, in a more complicated model, one could also net out the personal tax costs associated with interest income. Finally, see Altshuler and Newlon (1993) for the marginal tax costs of repatriations when there are also withholding taxes.

[8] In most situations the income from the high- and low-tax country would be summed and treated as income from one "basket", with $\tau_{\text{For}} = (4 \times 25\% + 2 \times 45\%)/6 = 31.67\%$. I treat the countries separately in this example to highlight how income from one country can lead to FTCs that shield income repatriated from another country.

are both positive (row (5)). In this case, a portion of domestic interest is allocated to foreign source income, thereby reducing the benefit of a dollar of interest by the ratio of foreign assets to worldwide assets. (Recall that this allocated interest will not reduce Tax_{For}.) The allocation of domestic interest reduces the incentive of an excess credit firm to issue domestic debt, especially when the firm has substantial foreign assets. Altshuler and Mintz (1995) note that more than 60% of firms were excess credit during the late 1980s, so interest allocation is potentially important.

Prediction 11 Due to interest allocation, the tax benefit of domestic interest deductions declines with the probability that a firm will operate as excess credit and with the proportion of assets held in foreign subsidiaries.

The analysis can be modified to examine the tax incentives associated with the parent supplying the foreign subsidiary with internal debt. The incentive is similar to that for external foreign debt shown in the rightmost column in Table 2.1, with one difference: with internal debt, the interest is taxable to the parent at rate τ_{US} when $\text{Tax}_{\text{US}} > 0$, so in some cases τ_{US} should be added in the rightmost column. Specifically, if the debt is internal rather than external, the entries in the rightmost column are $-\tau_{\text{For}}, +\tau_{\text{US}}$, 0, 0, $\tau_{\text{US}} - \tau_{\text{For}}$, and $\tau_{\text{US}} - \tau_{\text{For}}$ in rows (1)–(6), respectively. (Recall that a negative term means tax savings.) First consider the deficit credit case (row (4)) where the tax incentive to fund a foreign subsidiary with internal debt is nil: there is no tax incentive to use internal debt because the net benefit of deducting in the foreign country is exactly offset by the increased tax in the home country. In the excess credit case (rows (5) and (6)), the net tax benefit is $\tau_{\text{For}} - \tau_{\text{US}}$. For these rows, the tax incentive to issue debt increases with τ_{For} but it is offset by taxes owed by the domestic parent. In row (2), when $\text{Tax}_{\text{For}} = 0$ and $\text{Tax}_{\text{US}} > 0$, there is a tax disincentive of τ_{US} per dollar of internal interest: the extra foreign interest does not further reduce Tax_{For} and yet there is a positive tax liability of τ_{US} on the remitted interest. In contrast, when $\text{Tax}_{\text{US}} = 0$ (rows (1) and (3)) using internal rather than external debt does not change the entries in

Table 2.1: there is no tax on the interest received by the parent because the firm otherwise has domestic losses.

Prediction 12 The tax incentive to fund a foreign subsidiary with internal debt generally increases with τ_{For}; however, this incentive is offset in several situations as shown in Table 2.1.

Prediction 13 The tax incentive to issue external foreign debt increases with τ_{For}, although this incentive can be affected by the relative taxation of interest and equity income at the investor level.

Note that the incentive to save on foreign taxes might be tempered by investor-level taxes along the lines suggested in Miller (1977).

Other than in this paragraph, the results in this section are derived for the case where the domestic parent operated under a classical tax system in which interest is tax deductible but equity payments are not. If instead there is an imputation or integrated tax system (like in the U.K., France, or many other countries), equity holders receive a credit for taxes paid at the corporate level, which partially or fully eliminates the double taxation of equity income. This at least partially reduces the net tax advantage to debt. For example, ignoring personal taxes, Cooper and Nyborg (1999) show that the value of a levered firm in an imputation tax system equals

$$V_{\text{with debt}} = V_{\text{no debt}} + \frac{(\tau_C - \tau_I)}{(1 - \tau_I)} D, \tag{2.1}$$

where τ_I is the rate of imputation tax. In a full imputation tax system, dividend recipients receive a tax credit for income taxed at the corporate level, which they can use to offset their personal tax liability. If imputation results in a full tax credit at the corporate rate, then $\tau_I = \tau_C$ in Eq. (2.1) and there is no tax advantage to debt. In a partial imputation system, stockholders only receive a partial credit for taxes paid at the corporate level, which is analogous to making equity (at least partially) tax deductible, which in turn reduces the net tax advantage of debt. I am not aware of research that investigates the following prediction.

Prediction 14 The tax incentive to issue debt decreases with the degree of dividend imputation dictated by the tax law under which a company operates.

2.2 Empirical evidence related to multinational tax incentives to use debt

Testing multinational tax hypotheses is difficult because the data are hard to obtain and noisy. Most of the international capital structure tests are based on implications found in row (4) and especially row (5) of Table 2.1. Table 2.2 summarizes some empirical evidence related to multinational debt policy.

With respect to Prediction 11 (due to interest allocation, the tax benefit of domestic interest deductions declines with the probability that a firm will operate as excess credit and with the proportion of assets held in foreign subsidiaries), Froot and Hines (1995) find that debt usage is reduced for excess credit firms, with the reduction proportional to the fraction of assets that are foreign. Altshuler and Mintz (1995) also show that the use of foreign debt increases with the proportion of assets held overseas (presumably because domestic interest would be allocated abroad). Newberry (1998) and Newberry and Dhaliwal (2001) find that the likelihood of issuing domestic debt is highest when a firm is not excess credit and when less interest is allocated abroad. A related prediction is that firms shift away from debt financing when interest is allocated abroad. Collins and Shackelford (1992) show that firms increase their use of preferred stock when domestic interest allocation is unfavorable. Froot and Hines (1995) point out that, unlike interest, lease payments are not allocable, and show that excess credit firms rely more heavily on leasing.

Several papers provide evidence with respect to Prediction 12 (the tax incentive to fund a foreign subsidiary with internal debt increases with τ_{For}) and Prediction 13 (the tax incentive to issue external foreign debt increases with τ_{For}, although this incentive can be affected by the relative taxation of interest and equity income at the investor level). Examining a cross-section of countries with differing foreign tax rates,

Table 2.2 Summary of predictions and empirical evidence for multinational capital structure

Prediction	Empirical Evidence
Firm uses less debt when it has accumulated FTCs.	None
Excess credit firms should have less incentive than deficit credit firms to use domestic debt. The incentive for excess credit firms to use domestic debt declines with the proportion of assets that are foreign. The incentive to use foreign debt increases in the foreign tax rate.	Debt usage declines when firm is excess credit. The reduction is increasing in the fraction of assets that are foreign (Froot and Hines, 1995). Likelihood of issuing domestic debt is highest when deficit credit and decreases as FTC limitations increase (Newberry, 1998 and Newberry and Dhaliwal, 2001). Excess credit firms' use of foreign debt increases in τ_{For} and in the share of foreign assets (Altshuler and Mintz, 1995). Debt ratios of foreign affiliates increase in τ_{For} (Desai et al., 2004 and Altshuler and Grubert, 2000).
If domestic losses, use foreign debt.	U.S. multinationals borrow in foreign subsidiary when they have domestic NOL carryforwards (Newberry and Dhaliwal, 2001).
Use a different financing source than domestic debt, especially when foreign assets are substantial. For example, use leases instead of debt because lease payments are not allocated to foreign operations.	Weak evidence that excess credit firms lease more than other firms (Froot and Hines, 1995). U.S. firms' incentive to finance with preferred stock rather than debt increases with proportion foreign assets (Collins and Shackelford, 1992 and Newberry, 1998).
Use internal debt infusion rather than internal equity to finance foreign subsidiary, especially when τ_{For} is high. Similarly, finance via royalty agreement rather than with equity.	Net internal borrowing by subsidiary from parent increases in τ_{For} (Desai et al., 2004). Increase royalty payments when cheaper than repatriating dividends (Hines, 1995).
Use transfer pricing to increase (decrease) cashflow to low (high) tax affiliate.	Multinationals overinvoice low-tax affiliates (Lall, 1973). Foreign-controlled U.S. firms' U.S. tax expense is inversely related to difference between the U.S. and global tax rate (Mills and Newberry, 2001).

Prediction	Empirical Evidence
Repatriate dividends when excess credit. Repatriation for deficit credit firms negatively related to $\tau_{\text{US}} - \tau_{\text{For}}$. Remit dividends from high- and low-foreign-tax firms simultaneously, to reduce potential domestic taxes.	Excess credit firms repatriate more than deficit credit firms, and repatriation by deficit credit firms is inversely related to the cost of doing so. (Hines and Hubbard, 1990) Most repatriated dividends are "cross-credited" (Altshuler and Newlon, 1993)
Borrow via U.S. subsidiary that is less than 80% owned by multinational parent.	Example: Ford Motor Co. set up domestic financing subsidiary of which it owned 75% (Scholes et al., 2002).
Use triangle arrangements between subsidiaries in foreign jurisdictions with different tax burdens to reduce domestic taxes owed on remittances.	Low-foreign tax subsidiaries invest in high-tax affiliate subsidiaries, who in turn remit funds to U.S. parent at low or zero domestic tax liability; or low-foreign tax subsidiaries are capitalized by high-tax affiliate subsidiary, so repatriations from high-tax subsidiary are assigned a foreign tax rate that is a mixture of the low and high tax rates (Altshuler and Grubert, 2000).

Desai et al. (2004) indicates that the net internal debt infusion into foreign subsidiaries increases with τ_{For} (Prediction 12). Newberry and Dhaliwal (2001) find that the propensity to issue bonds in foreign markets increases in τ_{For} (Prediction 13). Hines (1995) demonstrates that royalty payments increase when they are a cheaper form of repatriation than are dividends. Finally, Grubert (1998) finds that an increase in the price of one form of remittance does not reduce total payments. Firms hold the total constant and substitute between different forms of remittance, such as dividends, interest, or royalties.

With respect to Prediction 10 (the incentive $\tau_C(.)$ to finance with domestic debt decreases with accumulated foreign tax credits for deficit credit firms) and Prediction 14 (the tax incentive to issue debt decreases with the degree of dividend imputation), I am not aware of any research that explicitly investigates these issues.

Other than Altshuler and Mintz (1995), most papers use very general specifications to test for foreign tax effects or the influence of interest allocation. For example, when they are considered at all, separate terms indicating excess credit status, τ_{For}, or the ratio of foreign to worldwide assets are used, rather than interacting the variables in the manner suggested by the theory. Also, the sharper predictions are often ignored. Finally, I am not aware of any multinational tax research that directly links tax benefits to firm value. To the extent that data are available, variation across countries in tax rules and incentives provides a rich and under-researched environment within which to investigate how variation in tax rules affect $\tau_C(.)$ and, therefore, the financing decisions of multinational firms.

2.3 Other predictions and evidence about multinational tax incentives

Interest allocation can be avoided altogether if the domestic borrowing is performed by a domestic subsidiary that is less then 80% owned by the parent (although this subsidiary must allocate interest on its own books). I am unaware of any systematic research investigating this issue. Scholes et al. (2002) present an example describing how Ford Motor Co. implemented this strategy.

Besides directly altering where and whether it issues debt, there are many related mechanisms by which a firm might respond to multinational tax law. A company might alter its transfer prices (the prices at which goods and services are transferred between related entities) to shift income from the high-tax to the low-tax affiliate. Though transfer prices are supposed to be "arms-length prices," the rules are vague enough to allow wiggle-room. Properly designed, transfer pricing allows for tax-free dividend repatriation. Consistent with this means of reducing overall taxes, Lall (1973) finds that multinational firms overinvoice their low-tax Columbian subsidiaries. Mills and Newberry (2001) find that shifting income to foreign operations increases in the difference between the U.S. tax rate and the global tax rate. Alternatively, multinational firms can use "triangle schemes" in which one subsidiary is capitalized by or invested in by another affiliate subsidiary (Altshuler and Grubert, 2000). These schemes allow firms to optimally mix remittances from high- and low-tax subsidiaries in ways that reduce domestic taxes on foreign source income.

More generally, firms can time dividend repatriation to coincide with low overall tax cost to the parent and subsidiary. In particular, deficit credit firms owe U.S. tax when they repatriate dividends, so they have incentive to delay repatriation. In contrast, excess credit firms often do not owe additional tax upon repatriation. Taking debt versus equity choices as given, Hines and Hubbard (1990) find that excess credit firms repatriate more than do deficit credit firms, and that repatriation by deficit credit firms is inversely related to the tax cost of doing so. Altshuler and Newlon (1993) show that most repatriated dividends are "cross-credited"; that is, the parent firm simultaneously receives payments from both high- and low-foreign-tax subsidiaries, and can use the extra credits from one source to offset potential domestic taxes from another.

Cash Management Hartzell et al. (2006) argue that one reason that some U.S. companies have accumulated so much cash in aggregate is because of the repatriation taxes that they would have to pay if they were to bring the money back home; therefore, they hold large cash balances overseas. These tax incentives are in addition to precautionary and transactions costs explanations for holding cash. The authors find empirical evidence in support of all three explanations. In the case of taxes, they find that cash holdings increase in foreign income, with a much stronger effect for firms with high implicit tax burdens for repatriated earnings.

3

Taxes, LBOs, Corporate Restructuring, and Organizational Form

3.1 Theory and predictions

Under perfect capital markets, an MM analysis implies a null hypothesis that organizational form and restructurings are irrelevant to firm value. However, imperfections in the tax, legal, and information environments can create situations in which the form of the organization or restructuring can matter.

3.1.1 Leveraged buyouts

There is a tax incentive for corporations to use substantial leverage in the management buyout process. This flows directly from the predictions in Section 1 that high tax-rate firms have incentive to use debt and that the associated tax benefits add to firm value. LBOs are particularly interesting because they lead to a much larger increase in leverage than do most debt issuances. LBOs also can provide an opportunity to mark assets to market, thereby increasing depreciation and the associated tax savings.

Prediction 15 All else equal, the tax incentive to perform a highly-levered buyout increases with the firm's expected post-deal tax rate, $\tau_C(.)$.

3.1.2 Distressed reorganizations and Chapter 11

Tax incentives can affect distressed reorganizations. Distressed firms with substantial accumulated net operating losses (NOLs) have incentive to file Chapter 11 because it facilitates reducing debt ratios (Gilson, 1997). Chapter 11 allows the firm that emerges from bankruptcy to have unlimited use of the pre-filing NOLs to shield future income, as long as there is no change in ownership (i.e., a large change in the ensuing two years in who owns the firm's equity). Reducing the debt ratio during reorganization preserves debt capacity and decreases the likelihood of precipitating an ownership change by future equity issuances.

Prediction 16 The tax incentive for a firm to file Chapter 11 (versus a work-out), to better facilitate reducing its debt ratio in reorganization, increases with the firm's accumulated NOL carryforwards and its expected post-deal tax rate.

3.1.3 C-corporations vs. S-corporations

Taxes affect organizational form in general, not just reorganizations. When an entity operates as a common "C Corporation," revenues returned to investors as equity are taxed at both the firm and investor levels. The firm level taxation is at the corporate income tax rate, and the investor taxation is at the personal equity tax rate. The equity rate is often relatively low because equity income can be deferred or taxed at the relatively low capital gains rate. In contrast, partnership income is passed-through and taxed only at the investor level, at ordinary income tax rates. The tax burden is often disadvantageous to corporate form. For example, at current maximum statutory federal tax rates (Figure 1), in 2002 an investor would receive $0.604 in partnership income; in contrast, corporate equity payments would return only approximately \$0.52 (assuming equity is taxed at a 20% capital gains tax rate). There are, however, nontax benefits to corporate form that outweigh the tax costs for many firms. Gordon and MacKie-Mason (1994) argue that these nontax benefits are large, annually equaling about 4% of equity value. See Scholes et al. (2002) and Gordon and MacKie-Mason (1997) for details about nontax costs and benefits of corporate form. See Shelley et al. (1998) for discussion of the costs

---

Prediction 17 All else equal, the tax incentive to operate as a C-corporation (versus a partnership or S-corp) increases in $[(1 - \tau_P) - (1 - \tau_C)(1 - \tau_E)]$.

3.1.4 Divestitures and asset sales

Tax incentives can also affect the valuation, purchase and sale of assets. Alford and Berger (1998) argue that spinoffs are preferred by high tax rate firms when they shed assets that lead to taxable gains because spinoffs can be structured to avoid taxes to both the seller and buyer. In contrast, all else equal, sales are preferred when the transaction results in a loss because this loss can be deducted against corporate income. Moreover, when a firm sells an asset, the deal can be structured to benefit the seller or purchaser, possibly by financing the deal with debt (Erickson, 1998).

Prediction 18 There is a tax incentive for high-tax firms to shed assets in spin-offs when the deal is profitable and via sales when the deal is not profitable. When a firm acquires assets, high-tax firms have incentive to use "taxable deals" financed with debt.

3.1.5 R&D partnerships

Leasing allows a low-tax-rate firm to "sell" tax deductions to high-tax-rate lessors. Analogously, research and development limited partnerships (RDLPs) allow low-tax firms to sell start-up costs and losses to high-tax-rate investing partners.

Prediction 19 All else equal, low tax rate R&D firms should form research partnerships with high tax rate investors.

3.2 Empirical evidence

Kaplan (1989) and others investigate tax benefits in leveraged buyouts. LBOs provide large interest tax deductions and also can provide an opportunity for asset value to be stepped up to market value. Note that the tax benefit of $1 of interest does not necessarily equal the top statutory tax rate. The net benefit is less than the top rate if all of the LBO interest expense can not be deducted in the current year, if there is a personal tax penalty on interest income, or if there are nontax costs to debt. If he assumes that the net tax benefit of $1 of interest is $0.15 and that LBO debt is retired in eight years, Kaplan estimates that the tax benefit of interest deductions equals 21% of the premium paid to LBO target shareholders.[1] Kaplan also estimates that among firms electing to step up asset value, the incremental depreciation tax benefit equals 28% of the premium. I am not aware of any research that explicitly investigates whether the probability of choosing a highly levered form of reorganization increases with the expected post-deal MTR (Prediction 15).

Gilson (1997) shows that firms in Chapter 11 reduce their debt ratios more when pre-filing NOLs are large (Prediction 16). He concludes that firms file Chapter 11 (versus a workout) in part because of tax incentives: Chapter 11 status offers smaller transactions costs to reducing the debt ratio, thereby minimizing the chance of an ownership change that would result in the loss of pre-filing NOLs.

Research centered on tax reforms has linked taxes with organizational form. The Tax Reform Act of 1986 (TRA86) set corporate tax rates above personal income tax rates, and also equalized capital gains and ordinary tax rates, providing a natural environment to test Prediction 17. These tax rate changes made partnerships attractive by

[1] Graham (2000) accounts for the declining marginal benefit of incremental interest deductions and estimates that the gross tax benefit of debt equaled approximately one-fourth of firm value in the mid-1980s RJR Nabisco and Safeway LBOs.

greatly increasing the tax disadvantage to operating as a corporation. Scholes et al. (2002) point out that there was a huge increase in formation of S-corporations (which are taxed as partnerships) following TRA86. Gordon and MacKie-Mason (1997) show that the increased corporate tax disadvantage due to TRA86 resulted in a reduction in the portion of aggregate profits paid via (and assets held in) corporate form; however, the economic importance of this reduction was modest. Finally, Guenther (1992) investigates how corporations responded to the 1981 Economic Recovery Tax Act reduction in personal income tax rates, which increased the tax disadvantage for corporations. He finds that firms altered policies that contribute to the double taxation of equity payout: firms reduced dividends and instead returned capital by increasing the use of debt, share repurchases, and payments in mergers (which are often taxed as capital gains).

Ayers et al. (1996) study small firms and find that entities choose to operate as S-corps, rather than C-corps, when they experience losses in their early years of operation. These losses can immediately be passed through to S-corp investors, while C-corps must carry losses forward to offset future corporate income. The experiment of studying small firms is especially telling because small firms can generally choose between S- or C-corp form with little difference in cost or nontax considerations; therefore, the choice highlights tax incentives. Interpreting this result as strong tax evidence is somewhat clouded, however, because Ayers et al. do not find that the choice between C-corp and proprietorship/partnership form is affected by tax losses (though nontax considerations can affect this choice). Erickson and Wang (2002) argue that S-corps can be sold for more than C-corps because of favorable tax treatment. Finally, Hodder et al. (2003) conclude that banks convert to S-corp status to eliminate double taxation of dividends and to reduce the onerous burden of the AMT. Research investigating organizational form choices using micro firm- and owner-specific tax information would be helpful. Such papers would most likely require accessing confidential tax returns.

Scholes and Wolfson (1990) describe tax incentives that encouraged merger and acquisition activity in the early 1980s (following the 1981 tax act) and discouraged these activities after TRA86. They provide aggregate evidence that M&A activity surged in the early 1980s, and declined in 1987, consistent with tax incentives. See Scholes et al. (2002) for details of how acquisitions vary along the tax dimension depending on whether the deal involves C- or S-corporations, subsidiaries, spin-offs, carve-outs, etc.

Alford and Berger (1998) show that firms trade-off tax and non-tax considerations when choosing between spinoffs and asset sales (Prediction 18). The authors estimate tax benefits as a means of determining the size and nature of nontax costs and argue that adverse selection, moral hazard, and agency costs are all traded-off against tax benefits to influence how firms structure their deals. Erickson (1998) also demonstrates that the structure of deals is affected by tax concerns. He shows that the probability that a sale is structured as a "taxable deal," financed with tax-deductible debt, increases with the acquirer's tax rate; however, he finds no evidence that seller tax characteristics affect deal structure. Erickson and Wang (2000) find that the price of subsidiary sales can be affected by tax considerations. These authors show that premiums (and seller abnormal stock returns) increase when the sale is structured to allow a step-up in subsidiary basis, so that the acquiring firm receives additional depreciation tax benefits. Thus, contrary to a Modigliani and Miller prefect markets null hypothesis, tax considerations affect both the pricing and structure of asset sales.

While taxes appear to affect the structure and price of some deals, the tax-minimizing form is not always selected. Hand and Skantz (1998) argue that issuing new shares in equity carve-outs can avoid tax liabilities that occur when a firm issues secondary shares (at a price above the firm's tax basis in the shares). The authors determine that, relative to issuing new shares, secondary carve-outs increase tax liabilities by an amount equal to 11% of the carve-out IPO proceeds. Hand and Skantz are not able to identify benefits associated with secondary carve-outs that are large enough to offset the increased tax payment. Maydew et al. (1999) find that incremental taxes incurred when firms perform taxable sales (rather than tax-free spinoffs) amount to 8% of the value of divested assets. The authors argue that firms incur these tax costs 1) because they are smaller than the financial reporting benefits (e.g., larger financial statement earnings), and 2) when selling firms are cash-constrained (sales provide a cash inflow; swaps do not).

Shevlin (1987) investigates whether firms that perform R&D via partnerships have lower tax rates than firms that do R&D in-house (Prediction 19). Two notable features of Shevlin's careful experimental design are his use of simulated tax rates, and his specification of many explanatory variables in "as-if" form (i.e., defining right-hand-side variables for all firms as if they funded R&D in-house, to avoid the endogenous choice of in-house versus RDLP possibly affecting the variables' values). Shevlin finds that tax rates exert a significant, negative influence on the probability of choosing an RDLP in two out of three as-if regressions. Using an NOL dummy to measure tax incentives, Beatty et al. (1995) find that low-tax firms are more likely to finance R&D via a financing organization both before and after TRA86.

The Research and Experimentation Tax Credit has also influenced corporate R&D spending. In his economically-weighted regressions, Berger (1993) finds a positive market reaction to announcements affirming the tax credit. His regression coefficients indicate that three-fourths of the benefit of the credit accrues to shareholders, with the remaining one-fourth increasing product price and therefore flowing to employees or suppliers. This latter finding implies that the tax credit creates an implicit tax in the form of higher prices for tax-favored R&D activity and that this implicit tax offsets some of the intended benefit from the credit (in other words, some of the R&D tax credit is passed along in the form of higher prices to suppliers of R&D inputs). Berger also detects a negative market reaction among firms that do not use the credit themselves but compete with firms that do. Swenson (1992) finds evidence consistent with low-tax-rate firms pursuing firm-specific R&D tax credits less aggressively than they are pursued by high-tax-rate firms.

Overall, this research indicates that tax considerations affect the structure and pricing of research and development activity in the United States. The cited papers investigate R&D spending associated with pre-TRA86 tax rules. I am unaware of any similar research that investigates the influence of the tax credit on R&D activity based on post-TRA86 rules (under which the credit is based on the R&D-to-sales ratio, rather than on nominal R&D spending). Moreover, the R&D tax credit has temporarily expired several times since 1986. It would be interesting to know whether these expirations have affected real R&D activity.

4

Taxes and Payout Policy

Modern dividend research began with Lintner's (1956) field interviews with 28 firms. Lintner found that dividends are stable, appear to adjust towards an earnings-payout target, and are rarely reduced. Miller and Modigliani (1961) provide the theoretical foundation of payout policy and conclude that dividend policy is irrelevant in a frictionless world with perfect capital markets. Research since that time has explored how market imperfections create an environment in which payout policy affects firm value. This section highlights tax incentives related to corporate payout policy. For brevity, I narrow the discussion to payout issues that parallel those in Section 1 or that shed light on unresolved capital structure issues (e.g., whether personal taxes affect security prices). See Allen and Michaely (1995, 2001) and Poterba (2001) for broad reviews of the various tax and nontax imperfections that can lead to payout policy affecting firm value and corporate decisions.

4.1 Theory and empirical predictions

Miller and Modigliani (1961) argue that in a perfect economic environment, firm value is determined by operating cash flows, not by whether a company retains or pays out profits, nor by the form of payout. This line of reasoning produces the null hypotheses for this section.

Null hypotheses

- Firm value is not affected by payout policy.
- Taxes do not affect corporate payout decisions.

Allen and Michaely (2001) show that the null can also hold if different classes of investors are taxed differently and firms have differing payout policies, as long as the marginal price-setter is tax-free.

Alternatively, firms can have a tax incentive to return equity capital via share repurchases rather than dividends if dividends are taxed more heavily than are capital gains for the marginal investor(s). Statements by financial executives that repurchases are a "tax efficient means of returning capital to investors" support this point of view (though Brav et al., 2005 conclude that taxes only play a second-order role in the choice between returning capital as dividends or repurchases).

If dividends are taxed more heavily than repurchases, there can be a negative valuation of dividends (relative to repurchased shares) (e.g., the CAPM with corporate and investor taxation in Brennan, 1970 or Auerbach and King (1983)). All else equal, if a firm were to increase dividends, the pre-tax return on its stock would need to increase so that after-tax returns do not change. This effect increases as dividend taxation increases relative to capital gains taxation.

Prediction 20 All else equal, tax effects imply that firm value is negatively related to 1) the portion of payout dedicated to dividends, and 2) dividend taxation relative to capital gains taxation. Analogously, required pre-tax stock returns increase with dividend payout and relative dividend taxation.

There are non-tax factors that also can lead to negative (e.g., reduced funds to pursue positive NPV projects) or positive (e.g., signaling or agency alleviation) dividend valuation (Allen and Michaely, 2001, see).

Note that dividend clienteles, in which high-tax rate investors own stocks with low dividend payouts, can occur under the null or

Prediction 20. Under the null, firms can have different payout policies that do not affect value, even if some investors are taxed more heavily on dividends (capital gains) and have a tax preference for capital gain (dividend) income. Similar clienteles can form under Prediction 20, based on the relative taxation of dividends and capital gains for different groups of investors.

To the extent that transactions are not costless, clientele tax characteristics can affect security prices. For example, the price of a stock changes from P_{cum} to P_{ex} as the stock goes ex-dividend. If the firm issues a dividend Div, its investors receive $Div(1 - \tau_{\text{div}})$ but simultaneously avoid capital gains taxes of the amount $(P_{\text{cum}} - P_{\text{ex}})\tau_{\text{cap gain}}$. With risk neutrality, continuous prices, and no transactions costs, and clienteles that do not vary before and after ex-days, Elton and Gruber (1970) show that $(P_{\text{cum}} - P_{\text{ex}})(1 - \tau_{\text{cap gain}}) = Div(1 - \tau_{\text{div}})$ in equilibrium, and therefore

$$\frac{P_{\text{cum}} - P_{\text{ex}}}{\text{Div}} = \frac{(1 - \tau_{\text{div}})}{(1 - \tau_{\text{cap gain}})}, \tag{4.1}$$

where $(P_{\text{cum}} - P_{\text{ex}})/\text{Div}$ is referred to as the ex-day premium.

Prediction 21 The ex-day premium reflects the relative taxation of dividends and capital gains for a given stock's clientele of investors.

Allen and Michaely (2001) call dividend clienteles "static" if they do not vary through time. Alternatively, if there are advantages to trade among differentially-taxed investors, dividend clienteles might be dynamic, which can lead to changes in the composition of the clientele around certain dates. Dynamic clienteles might lead to abnormally high volume around ex-days. For example, low-dividend-tax investors might buy stocks just before ex-day, capture the dividend, then sell the stock after it goes ex-dividend. Through this route, taxes might lead to ex-day behavior that produces trading volume but where the ex-day premium is close to one. Thus, Prediction 21 is a joint prediction about clienteles being static as well as tax effects.

Payout effects should vary with the tax rules of the country under consideration. For example, assuming static clienteles, the ex-day premium should increase with the degree of dividend imputation in a given country (because a tax refund for corporate taxes paid is attached to dividends in imputation countries, which reduces the effect of dividend taxation). The premium can be greater than one if imputation makes dividends tax-favored relative to capital gains (Bell and Jenkinson, 2002).

4.2 Empirical evidence on whether firm value is negatively affected by dividend payments

Boyd and Jagannathan (1994) test Prediction 20 by adding an (insignificant) dividend-yield as a right-hand side variable in the market model. In contrast, Litzenberger and Ramaswamy (1979) find a significant, positive dividend-yield coefficient. Kalay and Michaely (2000) emphasize that the positive dividend effect should show up in cross-sectional (because of cross-firm variation in dividend-payout) long-run returns (i.e., returns for stocks held long enough to qualify for capital gains treatment). They point out that Litzenberger and Ramaswamy (1979) use monthly returns, and allow high-dividend yield firms to be considered zero-dividend in non-dividend months. Kalay and Michaely (2000) do not find cross-sectional or long-run return evidence that high-dividend stocks earn a tax premium. Kalay and Michaely's findings imply that the effect identified by Litzenberger and Ramaswamy occurs for short-run returns, perhaps only during the ex-dividend week.

Fama and French (1998) test Prediction 20 by regressing (changes in) firm value on (changes in) dividends and "firm value if no dividends."[1] If personal taxes reduce the value of dividends, and one could design a clean statistical experiment that isolates tax effects, there should be a negative coefficient on the dividend variable in this specification. In contrast, Fama and French find a positive coefficient, which probably occurs because either their proxy for "firm value if no dividends" is measured with error and/or non-tax effects overwhelm the tax influence of dividends. For example, if firms use dividends to signal

[1] As discussed in Section 1.2.2, FF regress the excess of market value over book assets on dividends, interest and a collection of variables that proxy for V_U, with all variables deflated by assets. The variables that proxy for V_U include current earnings, assets, R&D spending, and interest, as well as future changes in earnings, assets, R&D, interest, and firm value. V_U is probably measured with error, which clouds interpretation of FF's results.

quality, dividend payments might be positively correlated with firm value. Or, if dividends are priced by tax-free investors, one would not expect a negative influence of dividends on firm value. Fama and French conduct the only study of which I am aware that directly regresses firm value on dividend variables in an attempt to determine the tax effect of dividends.[2]

4.3 Evidence on whether ex-day stock returns and payout policy are affected by investor taxes

4.3.1 Dividend clienteles

Prediction 21 is based on the existence of static dividend clienteles, so I start by reviewing dividend clientele research. Blume et al. (1974), Pettit (1977), and Chaplinsky and Seyhun (1987) provide weak evidence that investors hold stocks such that dividend yield is inversely related to personal tax rates; Lewellen et al. (1978) find no such evidence. However, these studies have poor measures for tax, risk, and wealth effects and therefore are hard to interpret. Auerbach (1983) concludes that tax-related preferences result in clienteles of investors that purchase stocks based on firm-specific dividend-price ratios. Scholz (1992) uses self-reported data from the 1983 Survey of Consumer Finances. This survey has information on retail investor stock holdings, a sophisticated measure of the investor's relative dividend and capital gains tax rates, household wealth, and self-declared risk preferences. Scholz finds a negative relation between the dividend yield for an investor's stock holdings and the relative taxation of dividends, which is consistent with a general preference for dividends by low-tax investors. Graham and Kumar (2006) investigate stock holdings and trades from brokerage house investors during 1991 to 1996. They find that retail investors as a group prefer nondividend paying stocks and institutions prefer dividend paying stocks. Within the class of retail investors, Graham and Kumar also find evidence of dividend clienteles. Low income (i.e., low tax rate) and older investors prefer dividend-paying stocks, and within the class of dividend paying stocks, older

[2] Another approach to study whether personal taxes affect asset prices investigates tax capitalization. See Section 1.4.1.

low tax rate investors prefer high yield stocks. They also find that high income retail investors decreased their dividend holdings when dividend tax rates increased in 1993.

Strickland (1996) finds that mutual funds and money managers hold low-dividend yield portfolios, while untaxed institutions such as pension funds show no preference. Dhaliwal et al. (1999) find that the percentage of shares owned by institutional investors increases by about 600 basis points in the year after a firm initiates paying a dividend.[3] Overall, there is weak evidence that the preference for dividends decreases with income tax rates – but no direct evidence that this preference leads to static tax-based clienteles.

Several papers link corporate actions to the (assumed) tax characteristics of their investors. Pérez-González (2000) classifies firms by whether their largest shareholder is an individual or an institution and finds that the former pay 30% fewer dividends than the latter. He also finds that when tax reform increases (decreases) the taxation of dividends relative to capital gains, firms with large retail shareholders decrease (increase) dividend payout. Poterba and Summers (1985) find a similar result for aggregate dividend behavior in the U.K. from 1950–1983. Lie and Lie (1999) also conclude that investor-level taxes affect payout policy. They find that firms with low-dividend payout (and presumably high-tax-rate investors) use self-tender-offer share repurchases more often than they use special dividends, and these firms also use open-market repurchases more often than they increase regular dividends.

Allen and Michaely (1995) point out that the trading volume around ex-days provides evidence about whether clienteles are static (which would imply that trading only occurs between investors in the same tax bracket, who always hold stocks with the same dividend characteristics) or dynamic (in which case there might be advantages to trade among differentially-taxed investors, potentially involving dividend-capture or arbitrage by low-dividend-tax investors). In the static case, there should be no abnormal volume because there are no abnormal

[3] See Del Guercio (1996) and Brav and Heaton (1997) for evidence that institutional investors favor high-dividend stocks for nontax reasons like prudent-man regulations.

advantages to trade around the ex-day. Grundy (1985), Lakonishok and Vermaelen (1986), and Michaely and Vila (1996) find evidence of abnormal trading volume on the ex-day, which is consistent with dynamic tax-related trading on the ex-day. Dhaliwal and Li (2006) find evidence of excess volume around ex-days, which they attribute to tax-motivated trading.[4]

4.3.2 Ex-day premia and returns

Elton and Gruber (1970) find that the ex-day premium was 0.78 on average in the 1960s, which they interpret to imply that dividends are priced at a 22% disadvantage relative to capital gains (Prediction 21). Moreover, the premium ranged from 0.70 (for the lowest dividend-yield decile of stocks) to 1.18 (for the highest decile), which is consistent with the highest (lowest) tax-rate investors purchasing the lowest (highest) dividend-yield stocks. The Elton and Gruber evidence is consistent with personal taxes affecting stock prices via dividend payout and dividend clienteles. Their findings are strengthened by Barclay's (1987) evidence that the premium was 1.0 in the early 1900s, before the advent of personal income taxes.

There are several complications to interpreting the ex-day phenomenon. Kalay (1982) points out that absent transactions costs and risk, arbitrage by tax-free investors should push the premium to 1.0. Kalay argues that transactions costs are too large for individual investors to be the marginal price-setters but instead zero-tax-rate institutions might fulfill that role at ex-day. Kalay's findings suggest that inferring tax rates from ex-day returns is complicated by transactions costs and the effect of institutional traders. Consistent with this view, Michaely (1991) finds that the mean premium equaled approximately 1.0 in both 1986 (when capital gains tax rates were much lower than dividend tax rates for wealthy individuals) and in 1987–88 (when statutory dividend and capital gains tax rates were nearly equal),

[4] Koski and Michaely (2000) find that abnormal volume can be quite large on ex-days due to non-tax activity. In their case, Japanese insurance companies captured dividends for regulatory reasons, using nonstandard settlement procedures that allowed them to buy just before and sell just after the ex-day. Note, however, that this form of nonstandard settlement ended in 1989, so it can not explain abnormal ex-day volume in recent years.

and was relatively invariant across dividend yield deciles during these years. Michaely's evidence is not consistent with retail investor taxation affecting stock prices, suggesting that prices might have been set by institutional investors in the mid-1980s.[5]

Bali and Hite (1998) argue that discrete stock prices lead to patterns consistent with those observed by Elton and Gruber (1970). Suppose a $0.20 dividend is paid and, during the era when stock prices were divisible by one-eighth, the stock price drops by the largest increment less than the dividend: $0.125. This implies an ex-day premium of 0.625, which occurs in the absence of personal tax effects. Moreover, this effect is strongest for low dividend stocks. Bali and Hite's (1998) argument might explain some of the observed ex-day phenomenon, however, it does not explain abnormal volume on the ex-day, which Michaely and Vila (1996) argue is evidence of tax-motivated trading.

Frank and Jagannathan (1998) argue that dividends are a nuisance, and that market makers are well- situated to handle their collection and reinvestment. Therefore, investors unload the stock cum-dividend to market makers, who are compensated for handling the dividend by the dividend itself. This is especially true for low-dividend stocks, for which the nuisance remains relatively the same but for which the reward for handling the dividend is smallest. The implication is that prices should fall by less than the dividend in part because transactions are at the bid when the market-maker buys the stock on the cum date and are at the ask when the market-maker sells the stock ex-dividend, and in part due to reduced demand on the cum-date. They find evidence consistent with their arguments on the Hong Kong exchange, where the average premium is approximately one-half during 1980–1993, even though dividends and capital gains are not taxed at the personal level. Kadapakkam (2000) strengthens this argument by showing that when the nuisance of handling dividends (i.e., cumbersome physical settlement procedures) was greatly reduced with the onset

[5] This discussion ignores the effect of risk (Michaely and Vila, 1995, see) and transactions costs (see Boyd and Jagannathan, 1994, Michaely and Vila (1996), and Michaely et al. (1996)) on ex-day behavior. For example, Boyd and Jagannathan (1994) regress capital return on dividend yield and find a slope coefficient of one and a negative intercept. They interpret the negative intercept as a measure of transactions costs.

of electronic settlement, the premium in Hong Kong became indistinguishable from 1.0.

Graham et al. (2003) cast doubt on price discreteness (Bali and Hite) or bid-ask bounce (Frank and Jagannathan) explaining ex-day pricing in the U.S. These authors note that price discreteness and bid-ask bounce were greatly reduced as pricing increments changed from 1/8ths to 1/16ths (in 1997) to decimals (in 2001) on the NYSE. According to the price discreteness and bid-ask bounce hypotheses, the ex-day premium should have moved closer to one as the pricing grid became finer. In contrast, the ex-day premium got smaller (further from one), which is inconsistent with the price discreteness and bid-ask bounce hypotheses. Graham et al. do find evidence consistent with the original Elton and Gruber tax hypothesis, however. They find that the ex-day premium fell in conjunction with the 1997 reduction in capital gains tax rates.

Graham and Kumar (2006) find that low-tax rate (and older) investors purchase stocks just before they go ex-dividend, especially high dividend yield stocks, while high tax rate (and younger) investors wait until after the ex-day. This is consistent with clienteles of investors who have a preference for dividends actively acquiring dividends around the ex-day. They also find that among low market capitalization stocks, for which retail investors are plausibly the marginal price-setters, the ex-day premium is lower in absolute magnitude in stocks for which high tax rate investors dominate. This is consistent with the implication from Elton and Gruber (1970) that investor tax rates are impounded into ex-day stock returns, and in particular, low tax rate investors' tax rates are impounded into the ex-day returns of high dividend yield stocks.

Overall, it is not possible to unambiguously interpret the ex-dividend day evidence in terms of personal taxes, though some recent evidence is compelling. Green and Rydqvist (1999) provide convincing evidence of personal taxes being impounded into asset prices. Swedish lottery bonds are taxed like common stock with tax-free dividends (i.e., the coupon is tax-free and capital gains are taxed). Therefore, one would expect prices to be bid up cum-coupon (as high-tax rate investors purchase the bonds) and drop after the coupon is paid (with the drop leading to a capital loss deduction, which reduces taxes in proportion to the capital gains rate). Because the coupon is tax-free, the ratio of price drop to coupon should be greater than 1.0, reflecting the personal tax advantage of the coupon. Moreover, regulations prohibit coupon capture or arbitrage of the type that might be expected to force the ratio to 1.0, and unlike the case of stock dividends, frictions and price discreteness work in the opposite direction of the proposed tax effect. Green and Rydqvist (1999) find that the ratio of price drop to coupon averages 1.30 for Swedish lottery bonds, implying that the relative tax-advantage of coupons relative to capital gains is impounded into bond prices. They also find that this implicit tax rate declined as tax reform reduced the top statutory personal tax rate during the 1980s and 1990s. Florentsen and Rydqvist (2002) find that the ratio averages about 1.46 for similar lottery bonds in Denmark.

McDonald (2001) investigates ex-day behavior in Germany, where the dividend imputation tax system attached to most dividends a tax credit for corporate taxes (until this feature was repealed in late 2000). This tax credit means that dividends are more valuable to German investors than are capital gains, all else equal. McDonald shows that tax considerations imply that the ex-day premium should be 1.43 under these conditions. In his empirical work, McDonald finds that the average premium is 1.26, indicating that about 60% of the dividend tax credit is impounded into the ex-day price. He also finds that 55% (35%) of the tax credit is reflected in futures (options) prices. Finally, McDonald demonstrates that there is abnormal volume for the six days leading up to and including the ex-day, and that abnormal volume increases in the dividend yield. This is consistent with foreigners, who do not enjoy the German tax credit, selling the stock just before ex-day.

Bell and Jenkinson (2002) investigate the effects of a July, 1997 tax reform in the U.K. Prior to 1997, the imputation tax credit attached to dividends was such that tax-free investors received a full tax refund, even though they did not pay taxes on the dividend. In other words, a $1 dividend was worth more than $1 to tax-free investors. The tax reform eliminated imputation credits for tax-free investors, implying that a $1 dividend is now worth only $1 to these investors. Bell and Jenkinson show that tax-free institutions like pension funds own the majority of U.K. equities and argue that they therefore are the marginal price-setters. Bell and Jenkinson find that dividend valuation decreased after the tax reform effectively reduced the imputation tax benefit of dividends. It would be helpful if there were more research like this that exploits the rich variation in tax codes around the world.

Overall, some ex-day papers provide clear evidence that personal taxes affect asset prices. This conclusion is not unambiguous across all papers, however, because of potential non-tax explanations for abnormal ex-day returns. If these alternative hypotheses completely explain ex-day returns, then in these circumstances personal taxes are not impounded into stock prices. However, even if tax rates do not appear to affect stock returns directly, tax considerations might still affect financial markets if they increase trading volume.

The payout results have implications for capital structure research. If the marginal investor in equities is tax-free but the debt price-setter is not, then the personal tax penalty to using debt might be quite large. If the marginal investor in equities *and* debt is tax-free, there is no personal tax penalty associated with debt financing. Finally, if the marginal-price-setter for equities is taxable and his tax rate is impounded into stock returns, this reduces the personal tax penalty on debt relative to the Miller (1977) scenario. Understanding the tax characteristics of the marginal price-setter(s) in various securities is an important issue for future research.

4.3.3 Is corporate payout policy affected by investor dividend tax rates?

In May 2003 dividend tax rates for retail investors were reduced from as high as 38% down to 15%, and the top tax rate on capital gains was reduced from 20% to 15%. According to the theory, this tax cut should lead to greater dividend payout because it reduces the tax disadvantage of dividends relative to capital gains. Chetty and Saez (2005) argue that the tax cut led to increased dividend initiations, helping to reverse the dramatic reduction in the proportion of public firms paying dividends documented in Fama and French (2001). Julio and Ikenberry (2004) concur that the tax reduction is consistent with the reappearance of dividend-paying firms; however, they argue that the trend to initiate dividends was already in motion, at least to some degree, before the tax cut was announced.

Recent research shows that the tax cut led to increases in special dividends (Blouin et al., 2004), as well as to increases in dividend payments among those firms already paying (Chetty and Saez, 2005). Moreover, the tax cut reduced tax rates for retail investor taxable accounts but much less if at all for tax-favored accounts or institutions. Blouin and Carter (2005) find that "dividend boosts were increasing in the percentage of the corporation held by individual investors," and Chetty and Saez (2005) find that dividend changes were smallest in stocks for which the largest investor was an institutional type that was not affected by the tax rate reduction.

Brav et al. (2006) argue that some firms were "on the fence" about paying a dividend in the existing equilibrium, and the tax cut led these firms to initiate, but overall the tax effect was only marginal. This seems plausible because the May 2003 tax cut reduced tax rates for retail investors but not for taxable institutions; therefore, one would expect a first-order effect only if retail investors are first order important. They survey executives, who indicate that tax rates are a second-order concern, less important than several other factors such as investor profitability.

5

Taxes and Compensation Policy

5.1 Theory and empirical predictions

An MM perfect capital markets analysis would lead to a null hypothesis that compensation policy does not affect firm value absent market imperfections. There has been a great deal of research investigating how agency costs and informational asymmetry can drive a wedge between employee objectives and shareholder wealth, as well as how compensation policy can improve the situation.[1] Another group of papers investigates how the tax code can affect the choice of when and how to pay employees. Analogous to Miller's (1977) arguments about capital structure, Scholes et al. (2002) argue that to understand compensation policy, one must consider the tax implications for both the employer and employee. Scholes et al. show how different tax rates for the firm and its employees, or changing tax rates for either party, produce trade-offs between salary and bonuses, deferred compensation, compensatory loans, pension contributions, fringe benefits, and stock

[1] See Murphy (1999) for a broad review of compensation research including pay-performance sensitivity and linking salary, bonuses, and stock compensation to firm performance. See Core et al. (2003) for a review that focuses on using equity compensation to align executive and shareholder incentives.

option compensation. This section reviews compensation research most closely linked to taxes and corporate finance: the choice of salary versus equity compensation, the choice between incentive stock options (ISO) and nonqualified stock options (NQO), and, linking back to Section 1 of this paper, the trade-off between compensation deductions and debt tax shields.

The first tax issue is straightforward. Salary payments lead to an immediate deduction that reduces tax liabilities, while employee stock options lead to a corporate deduction only when the options are eventually exercised (if then – see below). Ignoring incentives and other nontax issues, the first compensation prediction is

---

Prediction 22 All else equal, the tax preference of paying salary compensation instead of option compensation increases with the corporation's tax rate because salary expense is deducted immediately and option expense is delayed.

The second tax issue involves the choice between paying employees with incentive versus nonqualified stock options. ISOs and NQOs are similar in most respects other than tax treatment, allowing researchers to isolate how tax imperfections affect corporate compensation decisions.[2] With ISOs, the firm never gets a tax deduction, and the employee pays capital gains tax on the amount the share price exceeds the grant price when the stock is eventually sold (assuming that the option is exercised at least 12 months after grant and the share of stock is sold at least 12 months after exercise). With NQOs, on the exercise date the firm gets a deduction equal to the amount by which the price upon exercise exceeds the grant price, and the employee pays ordinary income taxes on this same amount. The tax trade-off between incentive and nonqualified stock options amounts to comparing the relatively light burden of the employee paying capital gains taxes for ISOs

[2] Stock appreciation rights are similar except the net benefit is paid in cash, not shares of stock. With stock appreciation rights, the employee pays tax at ordinary personal tax rates on the cash benefit when it is paid, and the firm contemporaneously deducts the cash benefit.

to the net NQO benefit (i.e., the corporate deduction less the cost to the employee of paying taxes sooner and at a higher rate with NQOs).

Prediction 23 All else equal, when the corporation is taxed at a higher rate than the employee on ordinary income, nonqualified options are preferred to incentive stock options because they lead to lower "all parties" taxation of option compensation. Incentive stock options are generally preferred if the corporation has a low tax rate relative to the employees.

This section also investigates whether deductions from employee stock options serve as nondebt tax shields that substitute for the use of interest tax deductions by corporations. DeAngelo and Masulis (1980) argue that firms with substantial nondebt tax shields will use less debt. Among papers investigating this hypothesis, most find weak or no evidence that the traditional measure of nondebt tax shields (depreciation) crowds out debt tax shields (see Section 1). Section 5.2 reviews recent research that examines whether option deductions might serve the role of nondebt tax shields as laid out in DeAngelo and Masulis. I do not formally state this as a prediction because it is already stated in Prediction 2'.

Finally, restricted stock is a form of compensation that appears to be gaining popularity as a substitute for stock options (e.g., Microsoft's recent public declaration that it will begin using restricted stock extensively). With restricted stock, the employee is granted the shares of stock but is restricted from selling the shares for a prespecified period. Unless the employee elects (via Section 83(b) of the Internal Revenue Code) to pay ordinary taxes on the shares at the time of the grant, the employee pays ordinary income tax when the restrictions are lifted (typically after a vesting period of several years expires). The company receives a deduction of the same dollar amount opon which the employee pays tax, at the time the employee pays tax. As of this writing, one key difference relative to stock options is that with restricted stock the company *must* take a charge to earnings that is spread over the restriction period (the charge is fixed at the time restricted stock is granted and is based on APB Ruling #25 or the fair value as determined by FASB Ruling #123), while an earnings charge is not required with stock options. The other key difference is that stock options have little value unless the stock price increases, while restricted stock is worth the value of a share of stock, and so can have substantial value even if the price falls somewhat after the stock is granted. I am not aware of any empirical research that comprehensively investigates restricted stock.[3]

5.2 Empirical evidence

Several papers investigate whether corporate and employee tax status affect compensation choice, and draw mixed conclusions. Hall and Liebman (2000) assume that all firms pay the top statutory tax rate and find some evidence that the use of executive options increased as the corporate tax rate declined from the 1970s to the 1980s. This is consistent with Prediction 22 (the tax benefit of options increases as corporate tax rates fall because the forgone opportunity to deduct salary expense immediately is less important). However, when they allow for cross-sectional differences in tax rates and annual fixed effects, the Hall and Liebman tax coefficient becomes insignificant.

In contrast, Core and Guay (2001) examine stock-option plans for employees other than the top five executives. Non-executives hold two-thirds of outstanding compensation options. Core and Guay find that high tax rate firms grant fewer options, consistent with Prediction 22; however, they do not find evidence that low-tax rate firms grant more options. Finally, Klassen and Mawani (2000) find that among Canadian firms option use decreases with the corporate marginal tax rate, as in Prediction 22 (note that option compensation is not deductible for Canadian corporations, which only strengthens the incentive to deduct salary expense immediately). Overall, then, the evidence is weakly consistent with Prediction 22.

Several papers investigate whether corporate and employee tax status affect the choice between incentive and nonqualified options. Austin et al. (1998) assume that executives are taxed at the highest statutory rate and investigate whether high tax rate firms use NQOs. They use

[3] See Blouin and Carter (2005) and Knoll (2006) for recent research about the 83(b) election.

five different variables to measure the corporate tax rate and find that none of them are statistically related to the form of option plan. This conclusion is generally consistent with the finding by Madeo and Omer (1994) that low- rather than high-tax-rate firms switched from ISOs to NQOs following the 1969 Tax Act, opposite the tax prediction. I am not aware of research that provides evidence unambiguously consistent with Prediction 23.

Consistent with personal tax incentives, Huddart (1998) finds that some employees accelerated NQO option exercise in 1992, prior to the anticipated 1993 increase in upper income personal tax rates (from 31% to 39.6%); however, he concludes that only one-in-five employees took this action, indicating that nontax factors more than offset personal tax incentives in many situations. Goolsbee (1999) finds that in aggregate an abnormally large number of options were exercised in 1992, prior to the tax increase. Hall and Liebman (2000) note that Goolsbee defines abnormal based on a linear trend in exercise activity. When they instead consider the number of vested options and recent changes in stock prices, Hall and Liebman do not find that employees accelerated options exercise in anticipation the personal tax rate increase; nor do they find a delay in exercise in anticipation of personal tax rate reductions in the 1981 and 1986 tax acts.

Matsunaga et al. (1992) conclude that tax factors affect the disqualification of ISOs. An ISO plan is disqualified (i.e., treated as an NQO plan for tax purposes) if an employee sells her stock less than 12 months after exercising incentive stock options. A company might want to disqualify an ISO plan to receive the corporate deduction associated with NQOs if the corporate tax rate increases relative to the personal tax rate and/or if the ordinary personal rate falls relative to the capital gains tax rate, both of which happened after the 1986 tax reform. Matsunga et al. perform a careful "all parties" tax analysis and conclude that firms with the largest net benefit of disqualification were the firms most likely to disqualify.

Overall, there is only modest evidence that taxes are a driving factor affecting corporate or employee compensation decisions. This is perhaps surprising because popular press articles indicate that the size of the corporate deduction provided by NQOs is huge, completely eliminating corporate taxes for many large, profitable firms in the late 1990s (e.g., NY Times, June 13, 2000).[4]

Financial statement footnote information can help us understand whether the magnitude of option compensation deductions is sufficient to affect overall corporate tax planning and also to determine whether these deductions are inversely correlated with interest deductions (and therefore might explain why some firms use little debt). I gather information on the exercise and grant prices for all options exercised from 1996 to 1998 by employees of Fortune 500 firms (see Table 5.1). Assuming that all of the options are nonqualified implies that the corporate options deduction equals the difference between the exercise and grant prices of the exercised options. Note that these deductions appear on tax returns and reduce taxes owed to the government; they do not appear as a deduction on financial statements,[5] nor are they collected by Compustat. One could multiply these deductions by τ_C to estimate their tax value.

The average (median) Fortune 500 firm had \$85 (\$16) million of annual deductions resulting from employees exercising stock options during 1996–1998 (Panel A of Table 5.1). These numbers are skewed: the firm at the 90th (95th) percentile had \$185 (\$379) million in deductions. As a percentage of financial statement tax expense, the deductions average 50%. As a percentage of the amount of interest it would take to lever a firm up until there are declining benefits associated with incremental deductions (i.e., levering up to the kink in

[4] Hanlon and Shevlin (2002) present evidence about options deductions for NASDAQ 100 firms. Hanlon and Shevlin provide an excellent summary of the accounting issues related to options deductions.

[5] Option deductions do not reduce financial statement tax expense because the deductions are not treated as a permanent expense. Instead, the deductions are added to stockholders' equity.

Note that the discussion in this section applies to the vast majority of firm-years because historically corporations elected to present their stock option information using the intrinsic value method and therefore did not expense options and reduce net income or earnings per share, but instead presented the information in the financial statement footnotes (and never expensed the option compensation to reduce net income). In 2002 and 2003 several dozen firms announced that they would begin to expense option costs on financial statements (which has the effect of reducing net income on financial statements). In the current regime, corporations are now required to expense options. Note that the tax rules have not changed regarding options – this footnote simply discusses whether firms report options expense as a net income reducing item on financial statements.

Table 5.1 Corporate Tax Deductions Resulting from Option Compensation for Fortune 500 firms, 1996–1998

Panel A Fortune 500 1996–1998	Annual Option Deduction ($ million)	Deduction/Interest Expense	Deduction/Tax Expense
Mean	85.2	9.371	0.495
25th percentile	3.8	0.030	0.029
Median	16.1	0.153	0.097
75th percentile	58.1	0.585	0.283
90th percentile	184.7	1.800	0.632
95th percentile	378.6	4.088	1.136

Panel B Specific Firms	Option Deduction ($ million)	Interest Expense ($ million)	Tax Expense ($ million)	Deduction/ Interest Expense	Deduction/ Tax Expense
Dell Comp. (1997)	468.6	3.0	424.0	156.19	1.11
Intel Corp. (1998)	1185.7	40.0	3069.0	29.64	0.39
Dollar Gen. (1997)	57.8	3.7	87.2	15.36	0.66
GM (1998)	157.1	72.8	−44.7	2.16	−3.51
Circuit City (1998)	27.2	9.1	−15.0	3.00	−1.81

Option Deduction is the dollar amount of option compensation expense that a firm can deduct from its taxable income in a given year, which is calculated as the number of options exercised in a given year times the difference between the weighted average exercise price and the weighted average grant price. This calculation treats all exercised options as if they are nonqualified options. *Deduction/Interest* is the option compensation deduction divided by interest expense, where *interest expense* is from financial statements. *Deduction/Tax Expense* is the compensation deduction divided by tax expense, where *tax expense* is from financial statements.

the Graham (2000) benefit functions discussed in Section 1.2.3), the option deductions average 49%. Panel B of Table 5.1 shows the numbers for some specific firms. In the years shown in the table, option deductions are larger than interest deductions for Dell Computer, Intel, Dollar General Corporation, General Motors, and Circuit City. Moreover, options deductions are larger than tax expense for Intel, GM, and Circuit City.

Overall, the magnitude of the compensation deductions are large for some firms; however, they are moderate for many companies and therefore do not appear to provide the final answer to the puzzle of why some firms appear to be underlevered. Nonetheless, Panel C of Table 5.1 reveals that compensation deductions appear to substitute for interest deductions, and so at least partially address the puzzle. The Pearson

(Spearman) correlation coefficient between the magnitude of option deductions and the degree to which a firm appears to be conservatively levered (as measured by amount of interest it would take to lever up to the kink in the benefit function) is 0.33 (0.46).[6]

Two recent papers investigate whether option deductions displace the use of debt along the lines of suggested in DeAngelo and Masulis (1980), that is, to explore whether option deductions serve as a form of nondebt tax shield that might substitute for interest deductions (Section 1.1). Graham et al. (2004) find that the magnitude of option deductions is large enough to reduce the median MTR for Nasdaq 100 and S&P 100 firms from 34% (when option deductions are ignored) to 26% (when option deductions are considered) in 2000.[7] Documenting a reduction in MTRs is important because, as argued in Section 1.3.1, nondebt tax shields should reduce the use of debt to the extent that the NDTS alter the marginal tax rate. Graham et al. find that debt ratios are positively related to tax rates and negatively related to the amount by which option deductions reduce marginal tax rates (consistent with Prediction 2'). Similarly, Kahle and Shastri (2005) find that long- and short-term debt ratios are negatively related to the size of tax benefits from option exercise. Finally, Graham et al. show that firms that appear to use debt conservatively when option deductions are ignored appear significantly less underlevered when options are considered.

Overall, the evidence is consistent with managers substituting away from debt when their firm has substantial option deductions. It would be interesting for future research to investigate whether other nondebt tax shields play this role (e.g., R&D tax credits or foreign tax credits), especially in eras during which option deductions were less prevalent. One "secretive" source of such deductions is tax shelters, which are investigated in Section 7.

[6] One shortcoming of this analysis is that I measure the tax benefit of *realized* compensation deductions, which are not necessarily the same as the deductions that managers expect ex ante, when they plan their capital structure. Nor do I distinguish between ISOs and NQOs, although Hall and Liebman (2000) note that NQOs account for 95% of option grants. Future research should address these issues.

[7] In light of the large reduction in tax rates for some firms, it is surprising that (for tax reasons) some of these firms do not use more incentive and fewer nonqualified stock options. One reason might be restrictions on the total amount of incentive stock options that can be granted in a given year.

6

Taxes, Corporate Risk Management, and Earnings Management

If capital markets were perfect, there would be no benefit to corporate hedging because investors would be able to achieve the same outcome by hedging on personal account. The null hypotheses is therefore that corporate hedging does not increase firm value. And yet, the corporate use of derivatives (presumably) to hedge has increased enormously in the past decade. For example, OTC swaps increased from $11 trillion in 1994 to over $200 trillion by 2005 (http://www.isda.org/index.html). A large number of corporate finance research papers investigate which market imperfections create situations that can make corporate hedging advantageous.

Theory suggests that hedging to reduce volatility can reduce expected costs of bankruptcy (Smith and Stulz, 1985), reduce underinvestment costs by shifting funds into states where financing would otherwise be scarce (Froot et al., 1993), help offset conservative decision-making that results from employee risk-aversion Tufano (1996), and reduce the effects of information asymmetry between managers, investors, and the labor market (DeMarzo and Duffie, 1991 and Breeden and Viswanathan, 1998). Though narrower in scope, taxes can also provide an incentive to hedge. In this section, I review imperfections in the tax code that can lead to corporate hedging being beneficial and also explore how similar imperfections can provide an incentive to manage earnings.

6.1 Theory and empirical predictions

Smith and Stulz (1985) show that if the function that maps taxable income into tax liabilities is convex, a firm can reduce its expected tax liability by hedging to reduce income volatility. The tax function is generally convex because corporate income tax rates are progressive, though the degree of progressivity for positive income is small. The main form of progressivity occurs because profits are immediately taxed at a positive rate, while the tax reducing effect of losses is effectively spread through time via tax-loss carryforwards (after carrybacks are exhausted) and is only valuable in states in which the firm is profitable. Due to the time value of money, therefore, the tax function is convex because the present value tax benefit of $1 in losses is less than the tax cost of $1 in profits.[1] With a convex tax function, firms have incentive to use derivatives to shift taxable income from good to bad states to reduce volatility and expected tax liabilities.

Prediction 24 All else equal, the corporate incentive to hedge increases with the degree of tax schedule convexity.

The second tax incentive to hedge involves increasing debt capacity by reducing income volatility. To the extent that increased debt capacity leads to greater debt usage, it also leads to greater tax benefits and firm value. Alternatively, increased debt capacity might go unexploited, thereby reducing expected bankruptcy costs Smith and Stulz (1985). Ross (1997) and Leland (1998) argue that the former effect dominates and therefore that hedging increases firm value via the tax benefits of debt.

[1] The logic is that the government effectively holds a call option on corporate tax liabilities and writes a put on corporate tax refunds, the net value of which can be reduced by reducing volatility. That is, present value considerations from delayed tax refunds reduce the value of the government's written put, so on net the governmental call option on tax collections is more valuable. Reducing volatility reduces the value of the call and the government's claim on corporate earnings.

Prediction 25 There is a tax incentive to hedge because it increases debt capacity. When firms use this extra debt capacity, the tax benefits of debt increase.

Hedging with derivatives transfers income across states within a given time-period. In contrast, earnings management is usually thought of as smoothing income through time. Like the hedging case, tax function convexity can provide an incentive to smooth income.[2] However, tax incentives to smooth are more unidirectional: All else equal, companies prefer to delay paying taxes due to the time value of money. Moreover, if tax rates are expected to fall, tax incentives to delay income are strengthened. The following prediction summarizes three conditions that can lead to a convexity-like incentive to smooth that works against the incentive to delay income recognition:

Prediction 26 Unless one or more of the following conditions are met, there exists a tax incentive to delay recognition of taxable income: 1) the tax function is progressive, 2) net operating loss carryforwards and other deductions are less than fully valued due to limitations on use and the time value of money, and/or 3) tax rates are expected to increase.

6.2 Empirical evidence

Many empirical papers measure tax function convexity using variables based on the existence of NOL or tax credit carryforwards (Prediction 24). These papers regress corporate derivative usage on a proxy for convexity and several nontax right-hand-side variables, and generally do not find evidence that convexity affects the corporate use of derivatives (e.g., Nance et al., 1993 for Fortune 500 types of firms

[2] There are numerous nontax explanations for earnings management. Schipper's (1989) review notes that firms might manage earnings to reduce required returns by lowering earnings variance, to impress outside investors who value stock via earnings multiples, because executive compensation is tied to accounting numbers, and because insiders can not credibly convey private information via other means.

or Tufano, 1996 for gold-mining firms). Rather than proxying for convexity, Graham and Smith (1999) explicitly map out tax functions and find that they are convex for about half of Compustat firms, and that the average among these firms could save approximately $125,000 in expected tax liabilities by reducing income volatility by 5%. Graham and Rogers (2001) compare this explicit measure of tax function convexity to derivatives usage for a broad cross-section of firms and find no evidence that firms hedge in response to tax function convexity. In contrast, Dionne and Garand (2000) use regression coefficients from Graham and Smith (1999) to estimate convexity and find that hedging among gold-mining firms is positively related to estimated convexity.

Graham and Rogers (2001) use simultaneous equations to investigate the joint hedging/capital structure decision, to determine whether firms hedge to increase debt capacity (Prediction 25). In one equation they regress derivatives usage on variables, including debt ratios, that explain corporate hedging and in the other equation they regress debt ratios on variables, including derivatives usage, that explain debt policy. Graham and Rogers find that hedging leads to greater debt usage. For the average firm, hedging with derivatives increases the debt ratio by 3% and adds tax shields equal to 1.1% of firm value.

Overall, the empirical evidence suggests that the tax incentive to hedge because of tax function convexity is weak at best. The statistical evidence is stronger that the tax incentive to increase debt capacity leads to greater hedging – though the economic importance of this effect appears to be only moderate.

In terms of earnings management, very little research directly investigates the conditions that can lead to a tax incentive to smooth earnings, particularly with respect to the three conditions in Prediction 26. Scholes et al. (1992) find that firms delayed recognizing income in 1986 in anticipation of lower future tax rates.[3] Barton (2001) regresses a measure of earnings management (i.e., discretionary accruals) on a crude convexity variable. Barton's measure of convexity is the excess of a firm's marginal tax rate over its average tax rate (i.e., tax expense

[3] Shane and Stock (2006) show that the stock market failed to anticipate earnings management that shifts taxable income from a high tax-rate fourth quarter to a lower tax rate first quarter.

divided by taxable income); a positive number indicates a progressive tax function. Barton finds that the absolute value of discretionary accruals is positively related to this measure of convexity, which he interprets as evidence of income smoothing in response to tax incentives. Similarly, using a NOL based convexity variable, Pincus and Rajgopal (2002) find that profitable oil and gas firms use derivatives to smooth income in response to tax incentives. As with the corporate hedging evidence, tax incentives appear to be a second-order consideration, rather than a dominant influence on earnings management.

7

Tax Shelters

Tax shelters offer a means of reducing taxes that may displace traditional sources of corporate tax deductions. Three common characteristics of shelters are that they reduce tax liability without greatly altering financial statement information, they are shrouded in secrecy, and they are often shut down once detected by the Treasury.[1] Tax shelters can take many different forms, and the current "hot product" is always evolving. They usually exploit glitches in the tax system such as asymmetric domestic and foreign tax treatment or a situation in which income is allocated beyond economic income. In the short-run, before detection, shelters can create a money pump for some firms, with benefits far exceeding transactions costs and the probability-weighted cost of audit/detection. One could imagine a long-run equilibrium in which the benefits of shelters are competed away or greatly reduced but, as a class, their secretive nature and the proliferation of new products appears to make "short-run" benefits continue largely unabated for those who participate.

[1] The dictionary definition of tax shelters would include interest deductions on home mortgages. In this paper, I focus on a more narrow definition. Namely, activity that leads to corporate tax deductions that the government would halt if it were aware of the activity.

One type of shelter, the high-basis low-value variety, involves an untaxed foreign investor and a taxable domestic corporation both participating in a deal. The untaxed investor is allocated a large portion of the income from the deal and then exits the transaction in a manner that leaves a large economic loss. The corporation can deduct the loss against taxable income. To get a feel for the magnitude of the benefit, Bankman (1999) presents an example in which the corporation contributes \$11 million to a deal and receives \$10 million in property and a \$40 million deductible loss. Therefore, the company effectively pays \$1 million (plus maybe \$3 million in transactions costs and a small expected cost of being caught) for a tax benefit of $\$40\tau_C$ million.

Some recent research investigates tax shelters. Desai (2003) compares taxable income reported on financial statements to actual tax collections and detects a growing wedge between these two series. He argues that traditional explanations such as accelerated depreciation, stock options, and earnings management explain only a portion of the wedge. Desai concludes (p. 1) that new "enhanced opportunities for avoiding and evading taxes through cheaper, more sophisticated, and less transparent mechanisms"(i.e., tax shelters) explain at least one-third of the book-tax income gap as of 1998, and that the portion of the wedge explained by shelters is growing. Graham and Tucker (2006) examine a sample of nearly 50 tax shelter firms. The tax shelters in their sample are huge, producing deductions that average nearly nine percent of asset value. These authors find that companies that use tax shelters use less debt than nonshelter peers, which is consistent with shelter deductions serving as a nondebt tax shield that is substituted in place of debt, in the spirit of DeAngelo and Masulis (1980).

Schallheim and Wells (2006) measure nondebt tax shields based on the difference between taxes paid and financial statement tax expense in an attempt to capture the effect of "off financial statement"deductions such as accelerated depreciation, stock option deductions, tax shelters, and the like. This allows them to use a much larger sample than that in Graham and Tucker (2006). In contrast to results cited in previous sections that are based on traditional measures of nondebt tax shields, Schallheim and Wells find that tax spread is negatively related to debt usage.

Clausing (2003) and Bartelsman and Beetsma (2003) find substantial evidence of tax-motivated transfer pricing, often offsetting approximately half of expected increase in tax revenuew. Hines (1995) reviews literature that finds indirect evidence of transfer pricing. Finally, Desai et al. (2004) find evidence that multinationals relocate income to tax haven countries, in part to delay repatriation to high tax rate parents. See Graham and Tucker (2006) for references to other recent tax shelter research.

Some forms of shelters, such as the tax deductible preferred stock (MIPS) discussed in Section 1, receive positive rulings from the Treasury and go on to become accepted financial transactions. Further discussion of tax shelters is beyond the scope of this chapter. The interested reader is directed towards Bankman (1999), the source for much of the tax shelter discussion in this section.

8

Summary and Suggestions for Future Research

This paper reviews research related to how taxes affect corporate activities. The research often finds that taxes affect corporate financial decisions – but the magnitude of the effect is not always large.

With respect to capital structure, there is cross-sectional regression evidence that high-tax rate firms use debt more intensively than do low tax rate firms. There is also exchange offer evidence that indicates that debt tax benefits add to firm value. However, there is room for much additional research to improve our understanding of capital structure tax effects.

One gap is the lack of time-series evidence about whether firm-specific changes in tax status affect debt policy. Another important area for future research is to isolate the market value of the tax benefits of debt for the broad cross-section of firms. Additional research is also needed to explain the apparently conservative debt policy of many firms. Such analysis might investigate whether non-debt tax shields substitute for interest deductions – and help solve the "conservative leverage puzzle." Three such nondebt tax shields include employee stock option deductions, tax shelters, and accumulated foreign tax credits. Recent research indicates that the first two help to (partially) explain apparent underleverage in some firms. Keep in mind, though, that nondebt tax shields should only affect tax incentives to the extent that they affect the corporate marginal tax rate.

We have also only scratched the surface regarding tax-related leasing research. There is currently not much analysis of whether taxes affect the pricing and structure of lease (or other financial) contracts, analysis of whether leases and debt are substitutes for the lessee, or evidence about how lessor tax rates affect leasing. There is also little research into the effect of relative corporate and personal taxes on the aggregate demand and supply of debt. Unambiguous evidence about whether taxes affect debt maturity choices is also rare. Finally, all of this research should emphasize robust statistical treatment of standard errors and the economic importance of tax effects, in light of Myers et al. (1998) statement that taxes are of third-order importance in the hierarchy of corporate decisions.

Though intriguing in theory, the profession has made only modest progress documenting whether investor taxes affect asset prices and in turn affect the costs and benefits of corporate policies. There is strong evidence that personal taxes drive a wedge between corporate and municipal bond yields. There is also plausible evidence that the personal tax penalty on MIPs interest income is only modest, which might imply that the personal tax penalty on debt is only modest (relative to using equity) – but this implication needs to be verified. Several papers assume that companies have clienteles of investors that have similar tax characteristics, and then link these companies' policies to the assumed investor tax rates; however, it would be helpful to make these linkages more direct. In general, we need more market evidence about the importance of personal taxes affecting asset prices, the effective equity tax rate for the marginal investor(s), and information related to the identity of the marginal investor(s) between different securities. One level deeper, we also need evidence that corporate policies are altered in response to these investor tax influences on security prices. Some of this evidence will be hard to come by and might require access to confidential information or data from countries with unique data or institutional settings.

Progress has been made relating multinational tax considerations to corporate financing decisions, especially in terms of the use of debt by affiliated foreign entities when foreign tax rates are high. However, there is a need for research that highlights capital structure comparisons between classical and other tax systems and direct tests of multinational tax incentives, including the interaction of explanatory variables when appropriate (e.g., excess credit status interacted with interest allocation considerations). It would be helpful if excess (or deficit) credit tax position were measured more precisely than simply using current-period average tax rates.

Several studies link corporate payout policy to tax considerations. In particular, the ex-day stock return and volume evidence is consistent with investor tax considerations influencing asset markets. The Green and Rydqvist (1999) study of Swedish lottery bonds stands out in terms of presenting clean ex-day evidence documenting personal tax effects and serves as a model for future research that isolates tax effects. Unique insights into some payout issues might be provided by comparing payout policy in classical versus other tax systems. In addition, there currently is no convincing evidence that the interaction of investor tax characteristics and payout policy affect firm value and stock returns. Finally, there is a need for direct evidence that tax-based investor clienteles exist (i.e., that investors hold certain securities because of the investor's tax status and the form of payout) – because many of the payout hypotheses implicitly assume that such clienteles exist.

There is some recent evidence documenting tax motivated compensation payments (i.e., the choice between salary and options paid to non-executive employees), risk management (i.e., hedging to increase debt capacity and the tax benefits of debt), and earnings management. However, we need more "all parties, all deductions" research in these areas, as well as analysis of whether these forms of non-debt tax shields are substitutes for each other or for debt interest. We also need compensation studies based on firm- and employee-specific tax rates and the choice between ISO and NQO plans. Finally, to date there have been few direct tests of whether earnings management is related to progressive tax schedules, less than full valuation of accumulated NOLs and other deductions, and/or expectations of changes in future tax rates.

Some studies have documented that firms choose organizational form based on relative corporate and personal tax rates, that asset sales are structured in response to tax considerations, and that corporate bankruptcy and highly levered restructurings have tax implications. However, we need more evidence about the choice of corporate form using firm-specific data, evidence that firms choose ex ante to perform highly leveraged buyouts in response to tax incentives, and, in general, more evidence about tax incentives affecting corporate reorganizations, spinoffs, and other forms of restructuring.

Finally, while it is convenient for academic research to investigate these tax issues one by one, there is potential for large gains from investigating how these various policies and tax incentives interact from the perspective of a corporate financial manager or tax planner. Along these lines, some recent progress has been made investigating tax shelters. Additional studies that integrate the murky world of tax shelters into the overall tax planning environment would be helpful. Overall, there are numerous important areas in which careful research can contribute to our understanding of how the imperfections created by taxes affect corporate decisions and firm value.

Acknowledgements

I thank Roseanne Altshuler, Alan Auerbach, Alon Brav, Merle Erickson, Ben Esty, Mary Margaret Frank, Michelle Hanlon, Cam Harvey, Steve Huddart, Ravi Jagannathan, Mark Leary, Jennifer Koski, Alan Kraus, Ed Maydew, Bob McDonald, Roni Michaely, Lil Mills, Kaye Newberry, Maureen O'Hara, Jeff Pittman, Michael Roberts, Doug Shackelford, and Terry Shevlin for helpful comments. I also thank Tao Lin, Rujing Meng, and especially Vinny Eng and Krishna Narasimhan for excellent research assistance. I apologize to those who feel that their research has been ignored or misrepresented. Any errors are mine. A more focused version of some of the material in this paper appears in Graham (2003, 2006).

References

Alford, A. and P. Berger (1998), 'The role of taxes, financial reporting, and other market imperfections in structuring divisive reorganizations'. Working paper, Wharton School, University of Pennsylvania.

Allen, F. and R. Michaely (1995), 'Dividend policy'. In: R. Jarrow, V. Maksimovic, and W. T. Ziemba (eds.): *Handbooks In Operations Research and Management Science*, pp. 793–837. Finance 9, Elsevier North-Holland.

Allen, F. and R. Michaely (2001), 'Payout policy'. Working paper, Cornell University.

Almeida, H. and T. Phillipon (2005), 'The risk-adjusted cost of financial distress'. Working paper, New York University.

Altshuler, R. and A. J. Auerbach (1990), 'The significance of tax law asymmetries: An empirical investigation'. *Quarterly Journal of Economics* **105**(1), 61–86.

Altshuler, R. and H. Grubert (2000), 'Balance sheets, multinational financial policy, and the cost of capital at home and abroad'. Working paper, Rutgers University J Pub Econ, 2003!!

Altshuler, R. and J. Mintz (1995), 'U.S. Interest-allocation rules: Effects and policy'. *International Tax and Public Finance* **2**, 7–35.

Altshuler, R. and T. S. Newlon (1993), 'The effects of U.S. tax policy on the income repatriation patterns of U.S. multinational corporations'. In: A. Giovannini, R. G. Hubbard, and J. Slemrod (eds.): *Studies in International Taxation*, University of Chicago Press.

Alworth, J. and G. Arachi (2000), 'The effect of taxes on corporate financing decisions: Evidence from a panel of italian firms'. *International Tax and Public Finance* **8**, 353–76.

Andrade, G. and S. N. Kaplan (1998), 'How costly is financial (not economic) distress? Evidence from highly levered transactions that became distressed'. *Journal of Finance* **53**, 1443–1493.

Asquith, P. and D. Mullins (1986), 'Equity issues and offering dilution'. *Journal of Financial Economics* **15**, 61–89.

Auerbach, A. J. (1983), 'Stockholder tax rates and firm attributes'. *Journal of Public Economics* **21**, 107–127.

Auerbach, A. J. (2002), 'Taxation and corporate financial policy'. In: A. Auerbach and M. Feldstein (eds.): *Handbook of Public Economics*, Vol. 3, pp. 1251–1292, Amsterdam: Elsivier North-Holland.

Auerbach, A. J. and M. A. King (1983), 'Taxation, portfolio choice, and debt-equity ratios: A general equilibrium model'. *Quarterly Journal of Economics* **98**, 587–609.

Auerbach, A. J. and J. M. Poterba (1987), 'Tax-loss carry forwards and corporate tax incentives'. In: M. Feldstein (ed.): *The Effects of Taxation on Capital Accumulation*, pp. 305–338, University of Chicago Press.

Austin, J., J. Gaver, and K. Gaver (1998), 'The choice of incentive stock options vs. nonqualified options: A marginal tax rate perspective'. *Journal of the American Taxation Association* **20**, 1–21. (fall).

Ayers, B., C. Cloyd, and J. Robinson (1996), 'Organizational form and taxes: An empirical analysis of small businesses'. *Journal of the American Taxation Society* **18**, 49–67. (Supplement).

Ayers, B., C. Cloyd, and J. Robinson (2001), 'The influence of income taxes on use of inside and outside debt by small business'. *The National Tax Journal* **54**, 27–56.

Baker, M. and J. Wurgler (2002), 'Market timing and capital structure'. *Journal of Finance* **57**, 1–32.

Bali, R. and G. L. Hite (1998), 'Ex-dividend day stock price behavior: Discreteness or tax-induced clienteles?'. *Journal of Financial Economics* **47**, 127–159.

Bankman, J. (1999), 'The new market for corporate tax shelters'. *Tax Notes* **83**, 1775.

Barclay, M. J. (1987), 'Dividends, taxes, and common stock prices: The ex-dividend day behavior of common stock prices before the income tax'. *Journal of Financial Economics* **19**, 31–43.

Barclay, M. J. and C. W. Smith (1995a), 'The maturity structure of corporate debt'. *Journal of Finance* **50**, 609–631.

Barclay, M. J. and C. W. Smith (1995b), 'The priority structure of corporate liabilities'. *Journal of Finance* **50**, 899–917.

Bartelsman, E. J. and M. W. J. Beetsma (2003), 'Why pay more? Corporate tax avoidance through transfer pricing in OECD countries'. *Journal of Public Economics* **87**, 2225–2252.

Barthody, J. and C. Mateus (2005), 'Debt and taxes: Evidence from bank-financed small and medium-sized firms'. Working paper, Aarhus School of Business (Denmark).

Barton, J. (2001), 'Does the use of financial derivatives affect earnings management decisions?'. *The Accounting Review* **76**, 1–26.

Beatty, A., P. G. Berger, and J. Maglio (1995), 'Motives for forming research and development financing organizations'. *Journal of Accounting and Economics* **19**, 411–442.

Bell, L. and T. Jenkinson (2002), 'New evidence on the impact of dividend taxation and on the identity of the marginal investor'. *Journal of Finance* **57**, 1321–1346.

Benninga, S. and O. H. Sarig (1997), *Corporate finance: A valuation approach.* New York: McGraw Hill.

Berger, P. (1993), 'Explicit and implicit tax effects of the R & D tax credit'. *Journal of Accounting Research* **31**(2), 131–171.

Berk, J., R. Stanton, and J. Zechner (2006), 'Human capital, bankruptcy and capital structure'. Working paper, University of California Berkeley.

Black, F. (1980), 'The tax consequences of long-run pension policy'. *Financial Analysts Journal* **14**(7), 21–28.

Blouin, J. and M. E. Carter (2005), 'Restricted stock and the section 83(b) election'. Working paper, Wharton.

Blouin, J., J. Raedy, and D. Shackelford (2004), 'The initial impact of the 2003 reduction in the dividend tax rate'. University of North Carolina, Working paper.

Blume, M., J. Crockett, and I. Friend (1974), 'Stock ownership in the united states: Characteristics and trends'. *Survey of Current Business* **54**(11), 16–40.

Boyd, J. and R. Jagannathan (1994), 'Ex-dividend price behavior of common stocks'. *Review of Financial Studies* **7**, 711–741.

Bradley, M., G. Jarrell, and E. H. Kim (1984), 'On the existence of an optimal capital structure: Theory and evidence'. *Journal of Finance* **39**, 857–878.

Brav, A., J. R. Graham, C. R. Harvey, and R. Michaely (2005), 'Payout policy in the 21st century'. *Journal of Financial Economics* **77**, 483–527.

Brav, A., J. R. Graham, C. R. Harvey, and R. Michaely (2006), 'Dividends and taxes: CFO survey evidence'. *Journal of Financial Economics* **77**, 483–527. Working paper, Duke University.

Brav, A. and J. B. Heaton (1997), 'The economic effects of prudent man laws: Empirical evidence from stock ownership dynamics'. Working paper, Duke University.

Breeden, D. and S. Viswanathan (1998), 'Why do firms hedge? An asymmetric information model'. Working paper, Duke University.

Brennan, M. J. (1970), 'Taxes, market valuation and corporate financial policy'. *National Tax Journal* **23**, 417–427.

Brick, I. and S. A. Ravid (1985), 'On the relevance of debt maturity structure'. *Journal of Finance* **40**, 1423–1437.

Campello, M. (2001), 'Taxes and capital structure: Do Investors' taxes matter? Evidence from the tax reform act of 1986'. Unpublished Ph.D. dissertation, University of Illinois.

Chalmers, J. (1998), 'Default risk cannot explain the muni puzzle: Evidence from municipal bonds that are secured by U.S. treasury obligations'. *Review of Financial Studies* **11**, 281–308.

Chaplinsky, S. and G. Niehaus (1990), 'The tax and distributional effects of levereged ESOPs'. *Financial Management* **19**, 29–38.

Chaplinsky, S. and H. N. Seyhun (1987), 'Tax rationality and the demand for dividends'. Working paper, University of Michigan.

Chetty, R. and E. Saez (2005), 'Do dividend payments respond to taxes? Preliminary evidence from the 2003 dividend tax cut'. *Quarterly Journal of Economics* **120**, 791–833.

Clausing, K. A. (2003), 'Tax-motivated transfer pricing and US intrafirm trade prices'. *Journal of Public Economics* **87**, 2207–2223.

Clinch, G. and T. Shibano (1996), 'Differential tax benefits and the pension reversion decision'. *Journal of Accounting and Economics* **21**(1), 69–106.

Collins, J. and D. Kemsley (2000), 'Capital gains and dividend capitalization in firm valuation: Evidence of triple taxation'. *Accounting Review* **75**, 405–427.

Collins, J. and D. Shackelford (1992), 'Foreign tax credit limitations and preferred stock issuances'. *Journal of Accounting Research* pp. 103–24. (Supplement 1992).

Constantinides, G. (1983), 'Capital market equilibrium with personal tax'. *Econometrica* **51**, 611–636.

Cooper, I. A. and K. G. Nyborg (1999), 'Discount rates and tax'. Working paper, London Business School.

Core, J. and W. Guay (2001), 'Stock options plans for non-executive employees'. *Journal of Financial Economics* **61**, 253–287.

Core, J., W. Guay, and D. Larcker (2003), 'Executive equity compensation and incentives: A survey'. *Economic Policy Review* **9**, 27–50.

Cornett, M. and N. Travlos (1989), 'Information effects associated with debt for equity and equity for debt exchange offers'. *Journal of Finance* **44**, 451–468.

Dai, Z., E. L. Maydew, D. A. Shackelford, and H. H. Zhang (2006), 'Capital gains taxes and asset prices: capitalization or lock-in?'. Working paper, University of North Carolina.

Dammon, R. and L. Senbet (1988), 'The effect of taxes and depreciation on corporate investment and financial leverage'. *Journal of Finance* **43**, 357–73.

Dammon, R., C. Spatt, and H. Zhang (2001), 'Optimal consumption and investment with capital gain taxes'. *Review of Financial Studies* **14**, 583–616.

DeAngelo, H. and R. W. Masulis (1980), 'Optimal capital structure under corporate and personal taxation'. *Journal of Financial Economics* **8**, 3–29.

Del Guercio, D. (1996), 'The distorting effect of the prudent-man laws on institutional equity investments'. *Journal of Financial Economics* **40**, 31–62.

DeMarzo, P. and D. Duffie (1991), 'Corporate financial hedging with proprietary information'. *Journal of Economic Theory* **53**, 261–286.

Desai, M. A. (2003), 'The divergence between book and tax income'. In: J. Poterba (ed.): *Tax Policy and the Economy*, Vol. 17, Cambridge, MA, pp. 169–206, MIT Press.

Desai, M. A., F. Foley, and J. Hines (2004), 'A multinational perspective on capital structure choice and internal capital markets'. *Journal of Finance* **59**, 2451–2488.

Dhaliwal, D., M. Erickson, and R. Trezevant (1999), 'A test of the theory of tax clienteles for dividend policies'. *National Tax Journal* **52**, 179–194.

Dhaliwal, D., S. Heitzmann, and O. Li (2005), 'Taxes, leverage, and the cost of equity capital'. Working paper, University of Notre Dame.

Dhaliwal, D. and O. Li (2006), 'Investor tax heterogeneity and ex-dividend day trading volume – The effect of dividend yield and institutional ownership'. *Journal of Finance* **61**, 463–490.

Dhaliwal, D., R. Trezevant, and S. Wang (1992), 'Taxes, investment-related tax shields and capital structure'. *Journal of the American Taxation Association* **14**, 1–21.

Dionne, G. and M. Garand (2000), 'Risk management determinants affecting firms' values in the gold mining industry: New empirical results'. HEC working paper.

Dittmar, A. K. (2002), 'An analysis of capital structure and investment policies: Evidence from corporate divestitures'. forthcoming in *Journal of Business*.

Dotan, A. and S. A. Ravid (1985), 'On the interaction of real and financial decisions of the firm under uncertainty'. *Journal of Finance* **40**, 501–517.

Eades, K. and F. Marston (2001), 'Incentives for leasing: Evidence from the largest U.S. lessees and lessors'. Working paper, University of Virginia.

Eckbo, E. (1986), 'Valuation effects of corporate debt offerings'. *Journal of Financial Economics* **15**, 119–151.

Ekman, E. (1995), 'Taxation and corporate financial policy'. Working paper, Uppsala University, Sweden.

Elton, E. J. and M. J. Gruber (1970), 'Marginal stockholder tax rates and the clientele effect'. *Review of Economics and Statistics* **52**, 68–74.

Emery, D., W. Lewellen, and D. Mauer (1988), 'Tax-timing options, leverage, and the choice of corporate form'. *Journal of Financial Research* **11**, 99–110.

Engel, E. M. E. and E. Maydew (1999), 'Debt-equity hybrid securities'. *Journal of Accounting Research* **37**, 249–274.

Erickson, M. (1998), 'The effect of taxes on the structure of corporate acquisitions'. *Journal of Accounting Research* **36**, 279–298.

Erickson, M. and E. Maydew (1998), 'Implicit taxes in high dividend yield stocks'. *Accounting Review* **73**, 435–458.

Erickson, M. and S. Wang (2000), 'The effect of transaction structure on price: Evidence from subsidiary sales'. *Journal of Accounting and Economics* **30**, 59–97.

Erickson, M. and S. Wang (2002), 'The effect of organization form on acquisition price'. Working paper, University of Chicago.

Esty, B. (1998), 'The impact of contingent liability on commercial bank risk taking'. *Journal of Financial Economics* **47**, 189–218.

Esty, B., F. Qureshi, and W. Olson (2000), 'Iridium LLC'. Harvard Business School. case study No. 200-039, Rev. 3/27/01.

Fama, E. F. and K. R. French (1998), 'Taxes, financing decisions, and firm value'. *Journal of Finance* **53**(3), 819–43.

Fama, E. F. and K. R. French (2001), 'Testing trade-off and pecking-order predictions about dividends and debt'. *Review of Financial Studies* **15**, 1–33.

Farrar, D. and L. Selwyn (1967), 'Taxes, corporate policy, and return to investors'. *National Tax Journal* **20**, 444–454.

Florentsen, B. and K. Rydqvist (2002), 'Ex-day behavior when investors and professional traders assume reverse roles– the case of danish lottery bonds'. *Journal of Financial Intermediation* **11**, 152–175.

Frank, M. and R. Jagannathan (1998), 'Why do stock prices drop by less than the value of the dividend?: evidence from a country without taxes'. *Journal of Financial Economics* **47**, 161–188.

Frank, M. M. (2002), 'The impact of taxes on corporate defined benefit plan asset allocation'. *Journal of Accounting Research* **40**, 1163–1190.

Froot, K. and J. Hines (1995), 'Interest allocation rules, financing patterns, and the operations of U.S. multinationals'. In: M. Feldstein, James Hines, and R. G. Hubbard (eds.): *The Effects of Taxation on Multinational Corporations*, University of Chicago Press.

Froot, K., D. Scharfstein, and J. Stein (1993), 'Risk management: Coordinating corporate investment and financing policies'. *Journal of Finance* **48**, 1629–1658.

Geisler, F. (1999), 'Equity security investments: Evidence on tax-induced dividend clienteles'. *Journal of American Taxation Association* **22**(1), 1–17.

Gilson, S. C. (1997), 'Transactions costs and capital structure choice: evidence from financially distressed firm'. *Journal of Finance* **52**, 111–133.

Givoly, D., C. Hahn, A. Ofer, and O. H. Sarig (1992), 'Taxes and capital structure: evidence from firms' response to the tax reform act of 1986'. *Review of Financial Studies* **5**, 331–355.

Goldstein, R., N. Ju, and H. Leland (2001), 'An EBIT-based model of dynamic capital structure'. *Journal of Business* **74**, 483–512.

Goolsbee, A. (1999), 'What happens when you tax the rich? Evidence form executive compensation'.

Gordon, R. H. and J. K. MacKie-Mason (1990), 'Effects of the tax reform act of 1986 on corporate financial policy and organizational form'. In: J. Slemrod (ed.): *Do Taxes Matter?*, pp. 91–131, (MIT Press, Cambridge).

Gordon, R. H. and J. K. MacKie-Mason (1994), 'Tax distortions to the choice of organizational form'. *Journal of Public Economics* **55**, 279–306.

Gordon, R. H. and J. K. MacKie-Mason (1997), 'How much do taxes discourage incorporation?'. *Journal of Finance* **52**(2), 477–505.

Graham, J. and L. Mills (2006), 'Using tax return data to simulate corporate marginal tax rates'. Working paper, Duke University.

Graham, J. R. (1996a), 'Debt and the marginal tax rate'. *Journal of Financial Economics* **41**, 41–74.

Graham, J. R. (1996b), 'Proxies for the marginal tax rate'. *Journal of Financial Economics* **42**, 187–221.

Graham, J. R. (1999), 'Do personal taxes affect corporate financing decisions?'. *Journal of Public Economics* **73**, 147–185.

Graham, J. R. (2000), 'How big are the tax benefits of debt?'. *Journal of Finance* **55**, 1901–1941.

Graham, J. R. (2001), 'Estimating the tax benefits of debt'. *Journal of Applied Corporate Finance* **14**, 42–54.

Graham, J. R. (2003), 'Taxes and corporate finance: A review'. *Review of Financial Studies* **16**, 1074–1128.

Graham, J. R. (2006), 'Taxes and corporate finance'. In: B. E. Eckbo (ed.): *Handbook of Corporate Finance – Empirical Corporate Finance*, Amsterdam: Elsevier Science.

Graham, J. R. and C. Harvey (2001), 'The theory and practice of corporate finance: Evidence from the field'. *Journal of Financial Economics* **60**, 187–243.

Graham, J. R., E. Hughson, and J. Zender (1999), 'Stock market reactions to capital structure changes: Theory and evidence'. Working paper, Duke University.

Graham, J. R. and A. Kumar (2006), 'Do dividend clienteles exist? evidence on dividend preferences of retail investors'. *Journal of Finance* **61**, 1305–1336.

Graham, J. R., M. Lang, and D. Shackelford (2004), 'Employee stock options, corporate taxes and debt policy'. *Journal of Finance* **59**, 1585–1618.

Graham, J. R., M. Lemmon, and J. Schallheim (1998), 'Debt, leases, taxes, and the endogeneity of corporate tax status'. *Journal of Finance* **53**, 131–162.

Graham, J. R., R. Michaely, and M. Roberts (2003), 'Do price discreteness and transactions costs affect stock returns? Comparing ex-dividend pricing before and after decimalization'. *Journal of Finance* **58**, 2613–2637.

Graham, J. R. and D. Rogers (2001), 'Do firms hedge in response to tax incentives?'. *Journal of Finance* **57**, 815–839.

Graham, J. R. and C. W. Smith (1999), 'Tax incentives to hedge'. *Journal of Finance* **54**, 2241–2262.

Graham, J. R. and A. Tucker (2006), 'Tax shelters and corporate debt policy'. *Journal of Financial Economics*. Forthcoming.

Green, R. C. (1993), 'A simple model of the taxable and tax-exempt yield curves'. *Review of Financial Studies* **6**, 233–264.

Green, R. C. and B. Hollifield (2003), 'The personal-tax advantages of equity'. *Journal of Financial Economics* **67**, 175–216.

Green, R. C. and K. Rydqvist (1999), 'Ex-Day behavior with dividend preference and limitations to short-term arbitrage: The case of swedish lottery bonds'. *Journal of Financial Economics* **53**, 145–187.

Grinblatt, M. and S. Titman (2002), *Financial markets and corporate strategy*. Boston, MA: Irwin McGraw-Hill.

Grubert, H. (1998), 'Taxes and the division of foreign operating income among royalties, interest , dividends and retained earnings'. *Journal of Public Economics* **68**(2), 269–290.

Grundy, B. D. (1985), 'Trading volume and stock returns around ex-dividend dates'. Working paper, University of Chicago.

Guedes, J. and T. Opler (1996), 'The determinants of the maturity structure of corporate debt issues'. *Journal of Finance* **51**, 1809–1833.

Guenther, J. A. (1992), 'Taxes and organizational form: A comparison of corporations and master limited partnerships'. *The Accounting Review* **67**, 17.

Hall, B. and J. Liebman (2000), 'The taxation of executive compensation'. In: J. Poterba (ed.): *Tax Policy and the Economy*, Vol. 14, Cambridge, Massachusetts, MIT Press.

Hand, J. R. M. and T. R. Skantz (1998), 'Market timing through equity carve-outs'. Working paper, UNC Chapel Hill.

Hanlon, M. and T. Shevlin (2002), 'Accounting for tax benefits of employee stock options and implications for research'. *Accounting Horizons* **16**, 1–16.

Harris, T. and D. Kemsley (1999), 'Dividend taxation in firm valuation: New evidence'. *Journal of Accounting Research* **37**, 275–291.

Hartzell, J., S. Titman, and G. Twite (2006), 'Why do firms hold so much cash? A tax-based explanation'. Working paper, University of Texas, Austin.

Harwood, E. and G. B. Manzon (2000), 'Tax clienteles and debt maturity'. *Journal of the American Taxation Association* **22**, 22–39.

Henderson, C. B. (2001), 'The financing choices of large commercial banks'. Working paper, University of Texas, Austin.

Hennessey, C. A. and T. M. Whited (2005), 'Debt Dynamics'. *Journal of Finance* **60**, 1129–1165.

Hines, J. R. (1995), 'Taxes, technology, transfer, and the R & D activities of multinational firms'. In: M. Feldstein, J. R. Hines, and R. Glenn Hubbard (eds.): *The Effect of Taxation on Multinational Corporations*, pp. 225–248, Chicago: University of Chicago Press.

Hines, J. R. (1996), 'Altered states: Taxes and the location of FDI in america'. *American Economic Review* **86**, 1076–94.

Hines, J. R. and R. G. Hubbard (1990), 'Coming home to america: Dividend repatriations by U.S. multinationals'. In: A. Razin and Joel Slemrod (eds.): *Taxation in the Global Economy*, The University of Chicago Press.

Hodder, L., M. L. McAnally, and C. D. Weaver (2003), 'The influence of tax and non-tax factors on the organizational form of banks'. *Accounting Review* **78**, 297–325.

Hovakimian, H., T. Opler, and S. Titman (2001), 'The debt-equity choice'. *Journal of Financial and Quantitative Analysis* **36**, 1–24.

Huddart, S. (1998), 'Tax planning and the exercise of employee stock options'. *Contemporary Accounting Research* **15**(2), 203–216.

Irvine, P. and J. Rosenfeld (2000), 'Raising capital using monthly-income preferred stock: Market reaction and implications for capital-structure theory'. *Financial Management* **29**(2), 5–20.

Jensen, M. and W. Meckling (1976), 'Theory of the firm: Managerial behavior, agency costs, and ownership structure'. *Journal of Financial Economics* **7**, 305–360.

Julio, B. and D. Ikenberry (2004), 'Reappearing dividends'. *Journal of Applied Corporate Finance* **16**, 89–100.

Kadapakkam, P. (2000), 'Reduction of constraints on arbitrage trading and market efficiency: An examination of ex-day returns in Hong Kong after introduction of electronic settlement'. *The Journal of Finance* **55**, 2841–2861.

Kahle, K. and K. Shastri (2005), 'Firm performance, capital structure and the tax benefits of employee stock options'. *Journal of Financial and Quantitative Analysis* **40**, 135–160.

Kalay, A. (1982), 'The ex-dividend behavior of stock prices: A re-examination of the clientele effect'. *Journal of Finance* **37**, 1059–1070.

Kalay, A. and R. Michaely (2000), 'Dividends and taxes: A re-examination'. *Financial Management* **29**, 55–75.

Kane, A., A. J. Marcus, and R. L. McDonald (1985), 'Debt policy and the rate of return premium to leverage'. *Journal of Financial and Quantitative Analysis* **20**, 479–499.

Kaplan, S. (1989), 'Management buyouts: Evidence on taxes as a source of value'. *Journal of Finance* **44**(3), 611–632.

Kemsley, D. and D. Nissim (2002), 'Valuation of the debt-tax shield'. *Journal of Finance* **57**, 2045–2073.

Kim, C. S., D. C. Maurer, and M. H. Stohs (1995), 'Corporate debt maturity policy and investor tax-timing option: Theory and evidence'. *Financial Management* **24**, 33–45.

Kim, E. H. (1989), 'Optimal capital structure in miller's equilibrium'. In: S. Bhattacharya and G. Constantinides (eds.): *Financial Markets and Incomplete Information*, pp. 36–48, Totowa, NJ: Rowman and Littlefield.

Klassen, K. and A. Mawani (2000), 'The impact of financial and tax reporting incentives on option grants to canadian ceos'. *Contemporary Accounting Research* **17**, 227–262.

Klein, P. (2001), 'The capital gain lock-in effect and long-horizon return reversal'. *Journal of Financial Economics* **59**(1), 33–62.

Knoll, M. (2006), 'Restricted stock and the section 83(b) election: A joint tax perspective'. Working paper, Wharton.

Koski, J. L. and R. Michaely (2000), 'Prices, liquidity, and the information content of trades'. *The Review of Financial Studies* **13**, 659–696.

Kraus, A. and R. H. Litzenberger (1973), 'A state-preference model of optimal financial leverage'. *Journal of Finance* **28**, 911–922.

Lakonishok, J. and T. Vermaelen (1986), 'Tax-induced trading around the ex-day'. *Journal of Financial Economics* **16**, 287–319.

Lall, S. (1973), 'Transfer pricing by multinational manufacturing firms'. *Oxford Bulletin of Economics and Statistics* **35**, 173–195.

Lang, M. and D. Shackelford (2000), 'Capitalization of capital gains taxes: Evidence from stock price reactions to the 1997 rate reductions'. *Journal of Public Economics* **76**, 69–85.

Leary, M. and M. Roberts (2005), 'Do firms rebalance their capital structures?'. *Journal of Finance* **60**, 2575–2619.

Leary, M. and M. Roberts (2006), 'The pecking order, debt capacity, and information asymmetry'. Working paper, Wharton.

Leland, H. E. (1998), 'Agency cost, risk management and capital structure'. *Journal of Finance* **53**, 1213–1243.

Leland, H. E. and D. H. Pyle (1977), 'Informational asymmetric, financial structure, and financial intermediation'. *Journal of Finance* **32**, 2371–387.

Lemmon, M., M. Roberts, and J. Zender (2006), 'Back to the beginning: Persistence and the cross-section of corporate capital structure'. Working paper, Wharton.

Lemmon, M. and J. Zender (2001), 'Looking under the lamppost: An empirical examination of the determinants of capital structure'. Working paper, University of Utah.

Lemmon, M. and J. Zender (2002), 'Debt capacity and tests of capital structure theories'. Working paper, University of Utah.

Lewellen, W., K. Stanley, R. Lease, and G. Schlarbaum (1978), 'Some direct evidence on the dividend clientele hypothesis'. *Journal of Finance* **33**, 1385–1399.

Lewis, C. (1990), 'A multiperiod theory of corporate financial policy under taxation'. *Journal of Financial and Quantitative Analysis* **25**, 25–43.

Lie, E. and H. Lie (1999), 'The role of personal taxes in corporate decisions: An empirical analysis of share repurchases and dividends'. *Journal of Financial and Quantitative Analysis* **34**, 534–552.

Lintner, J. (1956), 'Distribution of incomes of corporations among dividends, retained earnings, and taxes'. *American Economic Review* **46**(2), 97–113.

Litzenberger, R. H. and K. Ramaswamy (1979), 'The effect of personal taxes and dividends on capital asset prices: Theory and empirical evidence'. *Journal of Financial Economics* **7**, 163–700.

MacKie-Mason, J. K. (1990), 'Do taxes affect corporate financing decisions?'. *Journal of Finance* **45**(5), 1471–1493.

Madeo, S. and T. Omer (1994), 'The effect of taxes on switching stock option plans: Evidence from the tax reform act of 1969'. *Journal of the American Taxation Association* **16**, 24–42. (Fall).

Mankiw, N. G. and J. M. Poterba (1996), 'Stock market yields and the pricing of municipal bounds'. NBER working paper 5607.

Masulis, R. W. (1980), 'Stock repurchase by tender offer: An analysis of the causes of common stock price changes'. *Journal of Finance* **35**, 305–319.

Masulis, R. W. (1983), 'The Impact of capital structure change on firm value: Some estimates'. *Journal of Finance* **38**, 107–126.

Masulis, R. W. and A. Korwar (1986), 'Seasoned equity offerings: An empirical investigation'. *Journal of Financial Economics* **15**, 91–118.

Matsunaga, S., T. Shevlin, and D. Shores (1992), 'Disqualifying dispositions of incentive stock options: Tax benefits versus financial reporting costs'. *Journal of Accounting Research* **30**, 37–76. (Supplement).

Maydew, E., K. S. Schipper, and L. Vincent (1999), 'The impact of taxes on the choice of divestiture method'. *Journal of Accounting and Economics* **28**, 117–150.

McDonald, R. (2001), 'Cross-border investing with tax arbitrage: The case of german dividend tax credits'. *Review of Financial Studies* **14**, 617–657.

McDonald, R. L. (2004), 'The tax (dis)advantage of a firm issuing options on its own stock'. *Journal of Public Economics* **88**, 925–955.

Michaely, R. (1991), 'Ex-dividend day stock price behavior: The case of the 1986 tax reform act'. *Journal of Finance* **46**(3), 845–860.

Michaely, R. and J. Vila (1995), 'Investors' heterogeneity, and volume around the ex-dividend day'. *Journal of Finance and Quantitative Analysis* **30**(2), 171–198.

Michaely, R., J. Vila, and J. Wang (1996), 'A model of trading volume with tax-induced heterogeneous valuation and transaction costs'. *Journal of Financial Intermediation* **5**, 340–371.

Michaely, R. and J.-L. Vila (1996), 'Trading volume with private valuations: Evidence from the ex-dividend day'. *Review of Financial Studies* **9**, 471–510.

Mikkelson, W. and M. Partch (1986), 'Valuation effects on security offerings and the issuance process'. *Journal of Financial Economics* **15**, 31–60.

Miles, J. and J. Ezzell (1985), 'Reformulating tax shield valuation: A note'. *Journal of Finance* **40**, 1485–1492.

Miller, M. and F. Modigliani (1961), 'Dividend policy, growth and the value of the firm'. *Journal of Business* **34**, 411–433.

Miller, M. H. (1977), 'Debt and taxes'. *Journal of Finance* **32**, 261–275.

Miller, M. H. and M. Scholes (1978), 'Dividends and taxes'. *Journal of Financial Economics* **6**, 333–364.

Mills, L. and K. Newberry (2001), 'The influence of tax and non-tax costs on book-tax reporting differences: Public and private firms'. *Journal of the American Taxation Association* **23**, 1–19.

Minton, B. and K. H. Wruck (2001), 'Financial policy, investment opportunities and the demand for external financing: Evidence from low debt firms'. Working paper, Ohio State University.

Modigliani, F. and M. H. Miller (1985), 'The cost of capital, corporation finance and the theory of investment'. *The American Economic Review* **48**, 261–297.

Murphy, K. (1999), 'Executive compensation'. In: O. Ashefelter and D. Card (eds.): *Handbook of Labor Economics*, Vol. 3, North-Holland, Amsterdam.

Myers, S., J. McConnell, A. Peterson, D. Soter, and J. Stern (1998), 'Vanderbilt university roundtable on the capital structure puzzle'. *Journal of Applied Corporate Finance* **11**, 8–24.

Myers, S. C. (1977), 'Determinants of corporate borrowing'. *Journal of Financial Economics* **3**, 799–819.

Myers, S. C. (1984), 'The capital structure puzzle'. *Journal of Finance* **39**, 575–592.

Myers, S. C. (1993), 'Still searching for the optimal capital structure'. *Journal of Applied Corporate Finance* **6**, 4–14.

Myers, S. C. and N. S. Majluf (1984), 'Corporate financing and investment decisions when firms have information that investors do not have'. *Journal of Financial Economics* **13**, 187–221.

Nance, D. R., C. W. Smith, and C. W. Smithson (1993), 'On the determinants of corporate hedging'. *Journal of Finance* **48**, 267–284.

Nayar, N. (2005), 'Does the tax advantage of debt really increase firm value?'. Lehigh University, Working paper.

Newberry, K. (1998), 'Foreign tax credit limitations and capital structure decisions'. *Journal of Accounting Research* **36**, 157–66.

Newberry, K. and D. S. Dhaliwal (2001), 'Cross-jurisdictional income shifting by U.S. multinationals: Evidence from international bond offerings'. *Journal of Accounting Research* **39**, 643–62.

Newberry, K. J. and G. F. Novack (1999), 'The effect of taxes on corporate debt maturity decisions: An analysis of public and private bond offerings'. *Journal of the American Taxation Association* **21**(2).

O'Malley, M. P. (1996), 'The effects of taxes on leasing decisions: Evidence from panel data'. Working paper, Board of Governers of the Federal Reserve System.

Parrino, R. and M. Weisbach (1999), 'Measuring investment distortions arising from stockholder-bondholder conflicts'. *Journal of Financial Economics* **53**, 3–42.

Pérez-González, F. (2000), 'Large shareholders and dividends: Evidence from U.S. tax reforms'. Working paper, Harvard University.

Pettit, R. R. (1977), 'Taxes, transaction costs and the clientele effect of taxes'. *Journal of Financial Economics* **8**, 419–436.

Pincus, M. and R. Rajgopal (2002), 'The interaction between accrual management and hedging: Evidence from oil and gas firms'. *The Accounting Review* **77**, 127–160.

Pinegar, M. J. and R. C. Lease (1986), 'The impact of preferred-for-common exchange offers on firm value'. *Journal of Finance* **41**, 795–814.

Pittman, J. and K. Klassen (2001), 'The influence of firm maturation on firms' rate of adjustment to their optimal capital structures'. *Journal of the American Taxation Association* **23**, 70–94.

Plesko, G. A. (2003), 'An evaluation of alternative measures of corporate tax rates'. *Journal of Accounting and Economics* **35**, 201–226.

Poterba, J. M. (1989), 'Lifetime incidence and the distributional burden of excise taxes'. *American Economic Review* **79**, 325–330.

Poterba, J. M. (2001), 'Taxation and portfolio structure: issues and implications'. In: L. Guiso, M. Haliassos, and T. Jappelli (eds.): *Household Portfolios*, Cambridge, Massachusetts, MIT Press.

Poterba, J. M. and L. Summers (1985), 'The Economic Effects of Dividend Taxation'. In: E. Altman and M. Subramanyam (eds.): *Recent Advances in Corporate Finance*, Homewood, Ill: Richard Irwin.

Rajan, R. G. and L. Zingales (1995), 'What do we know about capital structure choice? Some evidence from international data'. *Journal of Finance* **50**, 1421–1460.

Ross, M. P. (1997), 'Corporate hedging: What, why and how?'. Working paper, University of California, Berkeley.

Ross, S. (1977), 'The determination of financial structure: The incentive signaling approach'. *Bell Journal of Economics* **8**, 23–40.

Schallheim, J. and K. Wells (2006), 'Are firms really under-levered?'. Unpublished working paper. University of Utah, Salt Lake City, UT.

Schipper, K. (1989), 'Commentary on earnings management'. *Accounting Horizons* **3**, 91–102.

Scholes, M., P. Wilson, and M. Wolfson (1992), 'Firms responses to anticipated reductions in tax rates: The tax reform act of 1986'. *Journal of Accounting Research* **30**, 161–191. (Supplement).

Scholes, M. and M. Wolfson (1990), 'The effects of changes in tax laws on corporate reorganization activity'. *Journal of Business* **63**, 141–164.

Scholes, M. and M. Wolfson (1992), *Taxes and business strategy: A planning approach*. Englewood Cliffs, N.J.: Prentice-Hall.

Scholes, M., M. Wolfson, M. Erickson, E. Maydew, and T. Shevlin (2002), *Taxes and business strategy*. Englewood Cliffs, NJ: Prentice-Hall, 2nd edition.

Scholz, J. (1992), 'A direct examination of the dividend clientele hypothesis'. *Journal of Public Economics* **49**, 261–85.

Schulman, C., D. Thomas, K. Sellers, and D. Kennedy (1996), 'Effects of tax integration and capital gains tax on corporate leverage'. *National Tax Journal* **49**, 31–54.

Scott, J. H. (1976), 'A theory of optimal capital structure'. *Bell Journal of Economics* **7**, 33–54.

Seida, J. and W. Wempe (2000), 'Do capital gain tax rate increases affect individual investors' trading decisions'. *The Journal of Accounting & Economics* **30**(1), 33–57.

Shackelford, D. and T. Shevlin (2001), 'Empirical tax research in accounting'. *Journal of Accounting and Economics* **31**, 321–387.

Shackelford, D. A. (1991), 'The market for tax benefits: Evidence from leveraged ESOPs'. *Journal of Accounting and Economics* **14**, 117–145.

Shah, K. (1994), 'The nature of information conveyed by pure capital structure changes'. *Journal of Financial Economics* **36**, 89–126.

Shane, P. and T. Stock (2006), 'Security analyst and stock market efficiency in anticipating tax-motivated income shifting'. *The Accounting Review* **81**, 227–250.

Sharpe, S. and H. Nguyen (1995), 'Capital market imperfection and the incentive to lease'. *Journal of Financial Economics* **39**, 271–294.

Shelley, M., T. Omer, and T. J. Atwood (1998), 'Capital restructuring and accounting compliance costs: The case of publicly traded partnerships'. *Journal of Accounting Research* **36**, 365–378.

Shevlin, T. (1987), 'Taxes and off-balance sheet financing: Research and development limited partnerships'. *The Accounting Review* **62**, 480–509.

Shevlin, T. (1990), 'Estimating corporate marginal tax rates with asymmetric tax treatment of gains and losses'. *The Journal of the American Taxation Association* **12**, 51–67.

Shum, P. M. (1996), 'Taxes and corporate debt policy in Canada: An empirical investigation'. *Canadian Journal of Economics* **29**, 556–572.

Shyum-Sunder, L. and S. Myers (1999), 'Testing static tradeoff against pecking order models of capital structure'. *Journal of Financial Economics* **51**, 219–224.

Sick, G. A. (1990), 'Tax-adjusted discount rates'. *Management Science* **36**, 1432–1450.

Smith, C. and L. M. Wakeman (1985), 'Determinants of corporate leasing policy'. *Journal of Finance* **40**, 895–908.

Smith, C. W. and R. M. Stulz (1985), 'The determinants of firms' hedging policies'. *Journal of Financial and Quantitative Analysis* **20**, 391–405.

Stefanescu, I. (2006), 'Capital structure decisions and corporate pension plans'. Working paper, Indiana University.

Stohs, M. and D. Mauer (1996), 'The determinants of corporate debt maturity structure'. *Journal of Business* **69**, 279–312.

Strickland, D. (1996), 'Determinants of institutional ownership: Implications for dividend clienteles'. Working paper, Ohio State University.

Swenson, C. W. (1992), 'Some tests of the incentive effects of the research and experimentation tax credit'. *Journal of Public Economics* **49**, 203–218.

Taggart, R. (1991), 'Consistent valuation and cost of capital expressions with corporate and personal taxes'. *Financial Management* **20**, 8–20.

Tepper, I. (1981), 'Taxation and corporate pension funding policy'. *Journal of Financial Economics* pp. 3–51.

Thomas, J. K. (1988), 'Corporate taxes and defined benefit pension plans'. *Journal of Accounting and Economics* **10**, 199–237.

Trezevant, R. (1992), 'Debt financing and tax status: Tests of the substitution effect and the tax exhaustion hypothesis using firms' responses to the economic recovery tax act of 1981'. *Journal of Finance* **47**(4), 1557–1568.

Tufano, P. (1996), 'Who manages risk? An empirical examination of risk management practices in the gold mining industry'. *Journal of Finance* **51**, 1097–1137.

Wang, S. (2000), 'Optimal expected corporate marginal tax rate and leverage adjustments'. Working paper, Cornell University.

Warner, J. B. (1977), 'Bankruptcy costs: Some evidence'. *Journal of Finance* **32**, 337–347.

Williams, M. (2000), 'Tax clienteles, implicit taxes, and tax capitalization: Interaction of multiple clienteles in financial markets'. Working paper, University of California, Los Angeles.